Jesus

AND

Jiu Jitsu

THE RISE OF A WARRIOR OF GOD

Raiza Garcia

ENDORSEMENTS

"A gracious grip—Raiza grabs her reader with a masterful stroke and does not release until a chapter's completion, only to tighten more in the next chapter. She tackles hard life issues with simple grit that will reach many hurting today. Warning: You'll be sharpened as a true friend sharpens a friend; all in ultimate submission to Jesus!"
— Dawn O'Brien, media personality, Christian speaker, and MC

"No one's life is unscathed with pain or sorrow. As a matter of fact, the greater the pain or the suffering, the higher the phoenix rises.

This book is about the human spirit. It is the most powerful source that lies within us all. For some of us during this dark period, we discover our true life purpose. Raiza has found hers and that is to spread hope, God, and the power of humanity.

I admire Raiza's conviction and fortitude in helping and guiding our community. This is a must-read book!"
— Dewey Doan, founder of Kekoa Collective

"Our pastor once shared with us that he could best describe hell as being in 'sheer loneliness.'

It is through Raiza's written experience and her faith in God, her maturity in grace and endurance, that she was able to not only mend old relationships but continue to work towards building new ones. Possessing these qualities and living with these virtues are important not only to being a Christian but also as a practitioner of Brazilian jiujitsu. This story is a living testament of how to live faith."
— Jason and Dawn Estrella, founders of Hawaii JiuJitsu Foundation

"Seldom has a book hit me in such a way that compels me to read from cover to cover immediately. Raiza Garcia's _**Jesus and Jiujitsu**_ did exactly that. From carefree young adulthood, to brokenness and deep pain, and then to the healing transformation into a powerful mother and woman who is changing her world, Raiza's pure and honest description is not only a look into the heart of this new and wonderful generation, but also of the hope and calling that lies within their souls. It is a must-read, not only for the young adult, but for all ages."
– Cal Chinen, Moanalua Gardens Missionary Church & Transform Our World Hawaii

"Raiza Garcia is a woman who so many of us can relate to in her exhilarating book of her personal life's journey. Her honesty and willingness to share the most intimate moments in her life will bring you to tears, as you encounter the amazing freedom that comes to those who believe and recognize the hand of God! This book will build your faith and a call to action! Raiza continues to be an advocate for others, a faithful mother, a vital contributor to her church family, and most of all, a Mighty Warrior for God!"
– Pastor Caron Aquino, The Wave Christian Fellowship

"This book describes the healing power of faith and martial arts through Raiza's journey. Through these avenues, she has climbed her way to mental health and is now using this journey to empower at-risk youth…a true sign of a warrior. This is a must-read book for anyone walking through a difficult circumstance in life and wanting to find hope and inspiration."
– Sergio Esquivel, Cauliflower Collective

JESUS
AND
JIU JITSU

THE RISE OF A WARRIOR OF GOD

RAIZA GARCIA

XULON PRESS

Xulon Press
2301 Lucien Way #415
Maitland, FL 32751
407.339.4217
www.xulonpress.com

Printed in the United States of America.

ISBN-13: 978-1-54566-733-0

Isaiah 44:22
I've wiped the slate of all your wrongdoings.
There's nothing left of your sins.
Come back to me, come back. I've redeemed you.
(The Message Translation)

To my son's father,
You are an outstanding daddy, dad, and father.
I am grateful for this journey
we have been on from darkness to light.
You are the number one Pinterest Project Dad
and it is a blessing to watch how you
show up for, teach, and pour into our son.
Thank you for your blessing in
sharing our journey with the world
to a healthy co-parent relationship.
Ninjas for life!

This book is dedicated to my son,
Roland James, and my mother and father.
The three of you taught and showed me
what unconditional love is all about.
You are my blessings that helped bring
hope and joy when I had lost it all.
Agape Love Forever

Acknowledgments:

Jackie and Tara: My first responders, my sisters for life. I love you both so much, eternal treasures!

Josh, Keyah, Kat: Your reviews, edits, and revisions meant so much. When I wanted to quit, your help kept me going.

My family: Karina, Addie, aunts, uncles, cousins—love you all. You bring joy to R. J. and I every time we get to see you!

The Wave Christian Fellowship: Pastor Lance, Caron, Judy and Davie I love you all so much and am forever grateful for your spiritual teaching, mentoring and love. All my mighty sisters in Christ- Tammy, Sarah, Julie, Mandi, Auntie Bobby, Bernie, your prayers have been my life-line. God bless you all!

Margaret: You are a divine gift from God for so many. Your spiritual wisdom, love, training and leading me to know the greatest love of my life, Jesus Christ is something I could never return. God bless you and your mighty anointing.

Poole's and Ferraro's: Love you all and the lessons of grace and forgiveness we have walked on in this journey

Dojo families: Dean, Little John, Matt, Jason, Chris, Chris Gracie, and all the countless training partners I have had the pleasure to train with through the years, I cannot express my gratitude in words. During some hard days you helped me make it through. All things KeKoa Collective are awesome! Love you all!

My forever homegirls- Emilie, Melissa, Tab, Krissy, Shana, Elise, Leslie, Kate, Bianca-how blessed I am to have you in my circle. Love you all forever.

My students the past 14 years: I love you all so much, you each taught me more than I could ever teach you. All of you remain treasures in my heart.

To **all the kind people** I have met the past seven years, even just a friendly smile meant the world.

Spiritual gangster heroes of mine... Lisa Bevere, Christine Caine, Joby Martin, Shawn Bolz, Stovall Weems, Bill Johnson, Danny Silk, Todd White, Kris Vallotton, Banning Liebscher, and Mo Isom. Your books, blogs, podcasts, devotions, sermons have fed my soul and spirit in the loneliest times. Praise God for all that you do and your ministries.

Kim Walker-Smith: the voice from God that brought me through the darkest hours of my life. God bless you!

My past, current, and future Ekklesia's—Chris, Johanna, Carol, Leslie, —time in prayer with you all is gift.

Alicia and Tammy: Praying, brainstorming, sharing ideas and hearts all year- you are inspirations and true warriors of Christ!

Luke DeKneef: Book cover artist. Mahalo for your amazing gifts and talents. What you created is beyond anything I could have dreamed of. God bless you brother!

Last but not least... **My Lord and Savior Jesus Christ**—all Glory and Honor is yours in this powerful story of redemption. I am your warrior, eternally.

Table of Contents:

Foreword

G od has a way of connecting people at the perfect moment in time. While sitting in a local café in Pensacola, Florida, a group of women I had been doing a Bible study with for years were talking and praying when this young, spunky, and wavy-haired woman approached our table and began to pray with us. Her presence was powerful. We invited her to speak at our upcoming mentor training later that week. When she arrived at the training, she shared her stories of Hawaii and the volunteer work she was doing there in the areas of sex-trafficking awareness. I listened in awe. A kindred spirit! God had brought a soul sister into my life, at a time I desperately needed, and in the sweetest and most humbling way.

Together, and over the last year or so, Raiza has made a huge impact in my life. We have shared late nights and early mornings together via phone calls. Even over 4,000 miles apart, we live each day with the focus on bringing awareness, education, and restoration to those impacted by human trafficking. In our time growing together, I have learned Raiza has a backbone of scripture, she speaks in eloquence of her experiences, and has gently, but firmly, held my hand during my own healing process. As a survivor of sex trafficking, my own journey has been a rollercoaster and nothing short of amazing. Raiza has taken the courage to walk with me during the hardship and has helped me cultivate a mind-set of strength, courage, bravery, and resilience through her prayers and encouragement. She speaks life through her own story, and through the pages of this book.

To become a warrior of God is not an easy road to travel. God has graced Raiza's journey with favor and opportunity. She shows us how to armor up, and through her authenticity and transparency, we can join Raiza on the road less travelled by most, and claim our identity in Christ.

All the best,
Alicia Tappan
Survivor of Human Trafficking/Advocate for Human Trafficking Victims

Chapter 1

Who Is My God?

I love those who love me,
and those who seek me find me.
–Proverbs 8:17 (ESV)

Today, as a faithful believer of God, a daughter of the Almighty King of the universe, a follower of Jesus Christ, it is humbling to look back and reflect on my early adult life away from God and where He has brought me to presently. As the journey to follow Christ continues and evolves, it becomes difficult to even remember being the person I was before the Lord saved me and captured my heart. That young woman, with so much energy, love, and spirit, yet away from God, seems like a storybook character from a lifetime away. I floated around life achieving career goals, living for fun, and was as carefree as a Disney princess, like former boyfriends would call me. The rose-colored glasses I wore did not lend for much spiritual growth. Marching to my own drum, I was on the worldly pursuit of happiness and pleasure.

In the Christian world, the phrases "born again," "dying to oneself," and "walking with the Lord" are common concepts that are taught in sermons and in Bible study groups. Even secular people have heard these terms and probably wonder what they mean. These terms were blurry to me throughout my twenties, like most Christian theology. I did not have any real understanding of

1

the Word of God. I was an ordinary young woman who graduated from college and was making my way toward a career like many other women my age. I was on a course set to pursue my dreams in terms of life goals, both professionally and personally. However, what I least expected regarding my future was the radical journey God would take me on. Life took some twists and turns that I certainly never dreamed or thought of. This journey would bring light to my ignorance and reveal to me the greatness of Jesus. I was living a life that I thought I was in control of and on a certain path. There were aspirations for my personal and professional life that I had, but Jesus had different plans. I had everything I needed and more in my twenties: a career, a home, friends, family, hobbies, endless travels, etc. I was comfortable and happy. Therefore, the idea of seeking God was never a priority to me. And so the day I met Jesus face-to-face, as a broken 30-year-old woman in complete despair, my life was forever changed. Darkness was chased away with the true light of God.

> *When Jesus spoke again to the people, he said, "I am the light of the world. Whoever follows me will never walk in darkness, but will have the light of life."- John 8:12 (ESV)*

We all have certain people, places, and things that we think of when we hear the phrase, "count your blessings." At the beginning of my faith journey, I really did not understand that blessings were a divine gift from God, with a mission and plans. I thought a blessing was synonymous with "lucky." Great things happening or having great people in my life was only because I was lucky. It never occurred to me that there was a purpose in all of these people, places, things in my life. They were all part of the story God was writing for my life, equipping me for things in my future.

This journey of faith has taught me that a blessing comes from the one true God above, and chance has nothing to do with these great happenings or circumstances. God has a purpose and a reason for everything that happens in our life. I did not begin to understand that until my world was flipped upside down at the age of thirty.

> *From everyone given much, much will be required;*
> *and from the one for whom more is provided, all the*
> *more they will ask of him.–Luke 12:48 (TLV)*

My immediate family is at the core of these gifts. As a child of the '80s, I had a dreamy upbringing by the world's standards. My parents' love story as teenage sweethearts to a 40-plus-year marriage is an entire novel on its own. They built a life for my sister and I that provided great opportunity for us in a safe, loving home. This was something so crucial that I probably took for granted too often as a child or teenager.

As a Cuban-American immigrant, my father always worked hard to provide for his family. He sacrificed to achieve great professional success so our family's needs were always met, along with most of our wants. Although he did put so much into his professional career; he was always and still is there for his family. I remember him at all the piano recitals, school plays, basketball tournaments, swim meets, and more.

My parents mostly made sacrifices in their own social and personal lives. I know that they had friends when we were growing up; I just never noticed them spend much time with friends. They really focused on our family and creating a loving home where they were always available to their daughters. I do not even remember them having hobbies of their own while we were kids. Driving us to all of our activities seemed to be their hobbies. It was not until I was a young adult in my twenties that I even learned my father had received his brown belt in judo as a teenager. He rekindled his martial arts career after his children were out of the house and earned his blackbelt after a 25-year hiatus.

As a Generation Xennial, born in 1981, I was blessed with a childhood filled with memories away from screens. My teen years were spent in a world without the existence of social media. I always felt safe, loved, and appreciated by my family. Growing up, my parents really sheltered us from all the evils, despair, and problems of the world. I excelled academically, I was athletic, and I had a fun social life filled with many friends. My mom is a devout Catholic, so we were raised Catholic, too. Completing the Catholic sacraments of First Communion, Reconciliation, and Confirmation was a rite of passage where I did learn about God and Jesus. Despite all this, I honestly never felt God's presence growing up. God always seemed like this huge mysterious entity that was so holy and far out of my reach. Having a personal relationship with God was not something I ever thought I could have or would ever need.

My rebellious heart as a rule-breaker and rule-bender stems back to my teenage years. I was young and reckless in some ways, causing mischief and breaking rules. Sneaking out to parties, lying to my parents, and cutting school are just some of the defiant acts I was bent toward. Of course, this leaked into my partying college years. There were some wild times, and I am grateful that they happened during the very beginning of the social-media era. Does anyone remember Myspace? Yes, I was in college then, but I did not have a Myspace account, fortunately. So those times are memories for the people involved, and thankfully they are not a part of the World Wide Web today.

Similar to the famous parable from the gospel of Luke, The Prodigal Son, much of my first thirty years of life was spent in rebellion to God. In this parable, I see myself and the story of millions of other lost souls. Most importantly, this story reveals the heart of the Father in heaven, our Almighty God. Our Father in heaven has an open and unconditional heart and love for His lost

4

son. This is one of the most beautiful stories taught in the Bible. This parable teaches how even his rebellious son who left home to pursue worldly status, possessions, and came back destitute, was met by his father with open arms. His son had been gone and squandered his inheritance, and yet, the father still received him with love and celebrated his return. He does not shame his rebellious son for his poor decisions. Instead, he embraces him and welcomes his son home.

This is the same love and mercy that our Heavenly Father shows to us. I now know so much about the heart of my Heavenly Father through my life's experiences and studies of the Bible. It was one thing to accept Jesus as my Savior. That was easy, my life was hanging by threads at the age of thirty. I was in an unhealthy marriage, with a baby and a tumor fighting for space in my uterus. Suicidal depression overcame me. Only Jesus could rescue me from the shambles my life was in and piece it back together with love, grace, and mercy over time. However, making Jesus Lord and walking in obedience has been the progressive sanctification that will continue until the day I go home to the Lord in heaven. Reading and learning about God's comforting love for His rebellious sons and daughters in the story of the "Prodigal Son" has really given me another level of gratitude for my own dad. He is a blessing from God with the same heart for his two daughters and grandchildren. No matter the poor decisions we have made and continue to make, my mom and dad have always been there, with open arms of love and mercy for us.

As a fresh-out-of-college teacher, I was full of zeal and passion. I was ready to make a difference in my hometown of Pensacola, Florida, for my at-risk middle-school-aged students. I had no clue what I was getting into, especially at the age of twenty-three. I was smaller in stature and looked the same age as my students. My first year as a middle school teacher in a poverty-stricken neighborhood taught me more than I could ever write in words. I have never cried so much at a job. After that first year, I made a vow to myself that I have kept thirteen years later to never cry in front of students again. This school was a Title 1 school. This means that the majority of its students live in poverty, and a lot of adverse childhood experiences result from their home lives. My eyes, sheltered from the idealistic childhood I had lived, were opened so wide that year and the years to follow. Students cursed me, threw things at me, and refused to comply. I was even spit on by students. I watched and did my best to prevent countless violent fights among them, and it broke my heart to see so much pain and trauma manifested in the classroom day after day.

I am not a quitter, and I was determined to show these kids that there are adults who do care for them. As a result, I formed a special bond and connection with this population of at-risk youth for years to come. I loved being their mentor and cheerleader, and it was so gratifying to see them rise from the ashes of their circumstances. I was fortunate enough to win an amazing grant with colleagues called the Shooting Stars, funded by the Michael Jordan Foundation. This program allowed some of the staff to take twenty of the most rebellious students with leadership skills on a trip of a lifetime. We traveled to the Grand Canyon two years in a row with them. These students were my "Shooting Stars", and I still keep in touch with some of them, even after all this time. They will forever have a special place in my heart and in my prayer life.

Through these years of crafting my trade of teaching, I had some romantic relationships that were the foundation of my Achilles heel and cross to carry in the future. This was the beginning of my walk in the gruesome wilderness of dating. I bought into the worldly cycle of hook-up, shack up, break up, and then repeat with a few boyfriends in my twenties. This cycle is something I have heard the great Pastor Joby Martin, from the Church of Eleven 22, preach on many times. I was caught in the lie that so many believe. Go out with a guy, have fun, date, hook up, and then move into something serious. Just go with the flow and see what happens. I followed this destructive cycle all through my twenties, breaking guys' hearts, and also getting my heart broken and bruised. This was just a life-style I believed was "normal." I was aimlessly going into relationships and never once considered God's perfect design of courting and marriage. These relationships were far from what the Word of God teaches, yet nothing abnormal in my social circles or the message our culture promotes. It was just a cycle that I could not get out of; not that I had a strong desire for something different at the time. I was living in complete ignorance. I thought, "*If I get married that would be cool*," but I never intentionally thought about marriage in any of my previous relationships. It was about what felt good until it did not "feel" good anymore, and then—break up.

In the midst of my twenties, I was living in my hometown of Pensacola, Florida, in a beautiful home that I owned with a sweet and caring boyfriend. Yet something was missing. The heart and spirit for adventure and travel and seeing the world was just not being fully met. For years, I would go and travel during my breaks as a teacher. I visited many of the fifty states and countless National Parks. I had spent summers backpacking and traveling abroad, exploring cultures, cuisines, and majestic sites. I wanted to see more of the world, and I certainly did not want to live in my hometown forever. I began to feel that my relationship with my boyfriend was holding me back from that dream. I convinced myself that was the unsettling feeling that I battled with daily. Looking back now, nine years later, I know that was God's first real knock on my heart. He was seeking me, but I was still too blind to see and answer His call. It would take a couple of years and a real destructive heartbreak to understand what I was missing or searching for. Fortunately, with the Lord, He calls us multiple times in our life. God's pursuit is relentless.

> *Now Samuel did not yet know the Lord: The word of*
> *the Lord had not yet been revealed to him. The Lord*
> *called Samuel a third time, and Samuel got up and*
> *went to Eli and said "Here I am; you called me."*
> *–1 Samuel 3:7-8 (NIV)*

I did what I had done all through my late teens and twenties; I broke up with the great guy and *boom* there was another one right in front of me. This guy was a friend for many years. We first met in elementary school at Catholic Catechism class. I was the shy girl that was studious. I listened to the scary nuns and never went through the desks of the students whose classroom we sat in once a week in the evening. Tim, the boy, was one of the naughty boys who cut up with his friends in the back of the classroom taking pencils from the students' desks and throwing them in the ceiling to try and get them stuck when the nuns were not looking. We were opposites then, and although we became friends years later in high school, we remained opposites in many ways.

Tim was in the military, a handsome man and a good friend. I had even visited him while he was stationed in Europe one summer when I was backpacking with a friend. We kept in touch through the years and remained close friends. It was an unorthodox romance to say the least. He was spending a year in the remote island of Diego Garcia (somewhere far away in the Pacific Ocean), and I was still at home in Pensacola, Florida. We spent a year video-chatting on Skype (before Facetime and smartphones). I called his remote year on that beautiful island "summer camp." He worked from his dorm room, spear-fished, and sailed regularly. We wrote letters, sent care packages, and thought we were in love.

This was our season of dating and courting; it was virtual, not reality.

After his year on the island, he would be moving to Hawaii, and I would be going with him. I think we both had this dreamy idealistic idea of what life would be like with one another, and since we had been friends for so long, it just made sense that getting married would be easy. Reflecting on this now makes me laugh on how naïve we both were.

I packed up my household goods, put my house on the rental market, and prepared for a life of exploration as a military spouse in the land of "Aloha." I was excited and nervous all at the same time. The emotions were overwhelming. My adventurous spirit that had spent so many years traveling as a teacher could not wait to explore Hawaii and anywhere my future husband's career would take us. Simultaneously, leaving my family and lifelong friends was sad and difficult. Pensacola had always been my home base. I would travel and visit places, but always came home. Now, my home would be a continent and an ocean away from Pensacola. Gone were the sedentary, compliant, and mundane feelings I had from past relationships that kept me unsettled. I thought this was the answer a married life to Tim where we would travel and be happy. That was the answer to what I was missing and searching for. Boy, did I learn in a dramatic way that I was completely wrong.

Chapter 2

Covenant vs. Contract

Marriage is the beautiful design of the Almighty,
a great and sacred mystery-meant to be
a vivid example of Christ and his church.
Ephesians 5:33 (Passion Translation)

We landed in Hawaii and it was a dream come true. I had seen so many pictures, videos, and heard all the stories of the beauty of the island of Oahu, but it is nothing like a firsthand experience. The vibrant colors of the landscape, the cooling trade winds blowing, the sunshine, the mountains, and the ocean were intoxicating. It is a unique and remarkable beauty that rightfully makes this precious state a bucket-list tourist destination globally. I have known many people over the years who have traveled to Hawaii and saved for a long time just to experience it, and I understand why.

Tim's new co-workers greeted us with flower leis in hand. We were taken to the Hilton Hawaiian Resort on the beach in Waikiki, where we would stay for a few weeks until we found housing. There, the military took great care of us right from the start. I could not believe the stunning vistas from the hotel we resided in. The perfect sunny, warm weather and outdoor beauty had me in a state of awe that I still find myself continuously in while living in Hawaii years later. We landed in paradise; it was hard to fathom that this would be home for the next few years.

Hawaii was an easy place to fall in love with. The tranquil sounds and views of alluring beaches and mountains surrounding every place the eye can see are breathtaking. The endless adventures of snorkeling and surfing the ocean waves and exploring every mountain peak and forest filled me with excitement. We set out to leave no area of the island unturned. Looking back, I was actually falling in love with the state and the idea of this place being home more than the man I would marry. We started making friends, and I found a teaching job easily. Life was getting settled, and Tim and I were finally in the same place geographically. We never really "dated" or even had life together until this point. On top of this enormous change in our lives, we were also busy planning a large-scale wedding in Florida. It was going to be a dream wedding, the dream wedding my mom always wanted. It was to be held in one of the most romantic locations imaginable, St. Augustine, one of the oldest, charming towns in the United States. We would be married in the Cathedral Basilica of St. Augustine, a National Historic Landmark that is a top tourist attraction with its beautiful architectural design and ornate Spanish Renaissance décor from the 1790s. The stunning reception would be across the street on a rooftop overlooking the water, with live music and dancing under the stars with 200 friends and relatives.

At first, the planning was easy for Tim and I for the most part. Whatever my mom wanted or the wedding planner suggested, we consented to it. We really did not care about the details. In fact, if it had been my real dream wedding, it would have been at a beautiful destination location with just immediate family and close friends. As an easygoing daughter, I was simply going along with the plan. The ceremony would be beautiful, and the party sounded like so much fun. However, with all the wedding talk, what was not discussed much was the actual marriage. We spent our first year in

Hawaii having so much fun, exploring the island chain, making friends, and working, but we never talked about the real stuff that makes up a marriage. Neither of us were "spiritual" at the time, so beliefs, faith, and values were not discussed deeply. Future children and how we would raise them were not mentioned. Finances, extended family, potential sickness, career goals, or any important topic that a couple should be on the same page about before marriage were casual brief conversations. I can only speak for myself and say that I was just assuming all things would work out. Life was enjoyable and that was all we needed to get through. We were just going with the flow of life, living with each other, and getting ready for our big wedding, as well as his deployment that would follow.

The following scriptures teach exactly what we were not understanding in our preparation for marriage. The keys to success in a lifelong, loving partnership lie in these precious words of God.

> *For wives, this means being supportive of your husbands like you are tenderly devoted to our Lord, for the husband provides leadership for the wife, just as Christ provides leadership for the church... in the same way the church is devoted to Christ, let the wives be devoted to their husbands in everything. Ephesians 6:22-24 (Passion Translation)*

> *So every married man should be gracious to his wife just as he is gracious to himself. And every wife should be tenderly devoted to her husband. Ephesians 6:33 (Passion Translation)*

Without any spiritual anchor in the Word of God or Christ, we did not comprehend the kind of love that is talked about in these scriptures from Ephesians. Without knowing Christ and

His unconditional love and grace, we did not know how to give or receive that type of love. Today, as a faithful believer with a deep connection with Christ, I would gladly submit to the leadership of a Christ-centered husband that followed and believed in these scriptures, because I have experienced that kind of love from Jesus—unfailing, nonnegotiable, endless love. The kind of love that endures all storms of life and moves into eternal life.

During the wedding preparation time, I was anxious about everything. The wedding, the deployment, and living in Hawaii so far away from my friends and family in the East Coast while my husband would be away had me fearful. It did not seem right in my soul. Something was off as far as Tim was concerned as well; he really did not have any interest in the wedding planning. He just agreed with everything to be easy, but really there was something bothering him. He seemed distant, and anything to do with the wedding started to annoy him. He really showed no interest in discussing any of the plans. I felt like more of a nag than anything when I would bring up any wedding talk to Tim.

As the date of our wedding approached, he shared that he was having a change of heart. He expressed that perhaps we should not get married. I was stunned, but my mind was just thinking about everything that had gone into the wedding that was just a few weeks away. I was ignoring the fear and anxiety I was feeling about it all as well. We could not cancel the ceremony and reception in which so much planning and money was invested. There were so many guests invited who had made arrangements to travel and be part of our big day. It is almost humorous to look back now at how I was so oblivious to what he was saying. In my mind, it was not even about the marriage or relationship; I was focused on all of the money and planning that had gone into our wedding ceremony and reception and how embarrassing it would be to call it all off. I was arbitrarily believing that once the stress of the wedding planning was over everything would just work out. Although, he expressed his reservations, I just brushed them off as "cold feet" and the wedding went on.

Now after my walk with God for the past six years, I know what a covenant marriage is built upon and consists of. It is one with God at the center, a lifelong, fruitful relationship between a man and a woman. Marriage is a vow to God, to your spouse, and to your families to protect and honor unconditional love, reconciliation, and sexual purity while growing closer to one another and to God. A covenant is an eternal commitment with God. Since Tim and I were not connected to Christ or anything spiritually at the time, this kind of vow was something we were ignorant about. We were not prepared for a covenant marriage because neither one of us had a relationship with Jesus. Nothing about our time together pointed to a lifelong union.

It would be a contractual marriage that would let life happen and see where it went. We could always bail out and get divorced like many in the world do. This is the opposite of a covenant, because a contract gives us options to negotiate and leave. God was never a part of our commitment. We never talked much about God, besides sharing that we believed in him. As far as knowing the Lord, His character, praying for God's will, or having knowledge of the Bible, none of that was part of our story. Now looking back, with those crucial missing pieces, I understand why our marriage was set on a course for destruction.

The weekend of the wedding arrived and it was marvelous. It was the most beautiful October weather in Florida that a bride could ask for. The charming historic bed and breakfasts that would host our friends and family were perfect. The dresses were stunning. The flowers and decorations, all of it could have come straight from a wedding magazine. My parents were jubilant, and just seeing all the joy on everyone's faces was contagious. Friends and family members had traveled great distances to be part of our weekend. It was a beautiful reunion for many in attendance. Tim and I were thrilled to be around our lifelong friends and our families, since we lived so far away. It was a grand party, the entire weekend.

My dress was picture perfect, a whimsical off-white dress that I had bought at Kleinfeld Bridal in New York City, a designer dress from the famous "Say Yes to the Dress" store that is on television. My dad walked me down the aisle, with tears rolling down his face in the breathtaking cathedral. We approached my future husband at the altar. He was pretty drunk and I was not exactly sober myself. We leaned on one another during the long mass ceremony probably looking like a sweet, newly married couple, but in actuality, we were having trouble standing on our own two feet with all of the alcohol flowing through our bodies.

As we entered our dream rooftop reception, we danced and partied under the stars to a live band with all of our friends and family. It was and remains the most fun party I have been to. Everyone in attendance was filled with joy, there was no "drama' or arguments. We ate, drank, danced, and were merry. In fact, everyone in attendance was having such a good time that at midnight when it was supposed to be over, my mother decided she did not want the party to end and another hour of the reception was booked on site. Looking back, it seemed like everyone was out to enjoy themselves at a grand gala rather than celebrate the marriage union that had just occurred. I can still look back and reminisce on the fabulous party and how perfect it all was, even though the marriage did not work.

But in this was a great lesson: marriage is not about planning a wedding or a party. A marriage is a lifelong commitment with God at the center. We had it all wrong from the beginning.

We headed back to Hawaii to prepare for Tim's deployment a few weeks later. He was about to deploy to the Middle East for eight months. I had a great circle of friends, even some other military spouses whose husbands were deploying too. We had plans to train and run a marathon in Hawaii. We felt we would just run while our husbands were away and that is what I did, I kissed my husband goodbye at the airport and hit the pavement for eight months, accomplishing a lifelong goal of running a marathon on the North Shore of Oahu.

Chapter 3

The Break

*Even though I walk through the valley of the
shadow of death, I will fear no evil, for you are
with me; your rod and your staff, they comfort me.
Psalms 23:4 (NIV)*

My husband was not the same person when he returned from his overseas deployment. I assumed there would be some awkwardness in the transition back to life after being in the middle east on a base for eight months, but I was not expecting such a drastic change. I felt something had happened while he was away, and whatever it was, his affections toward me were different. Something seemed to bother him. His attitude and behavior toward me was indifferent and cold. I often felt that he did not want me around, I could not understand why. Different thoughts raced through my mind during that time. Was this post-traumatic stress disorder (PTSD) from being deployed? Had he done something while he was away? Was he having a hard time living with the guilt? Did he cheat on me? Did he commit a crime? The thoughts made me crazy. They consumed me, yet I wasn't receiving any answers. I felt that I had to know what happened to the person I had married. There was little communication between us. As the months progressed, I became sad and lonely, feeling trapped in a life I did not sign up for.

With these new feelings of loneliness, I was desperate to find someone I could talk to about what was going on; someone who could help. My husband would not speak to me. I would walk into a room and try to start a conversation and he would walk away, as if I was not even present. Eventually, his consistent rejection left me with little desire to speak with him.

I was living in a dark tunnel with no light ahead of me. Depression crept up quickly. At the beginning, I struggled with little things such as my husband's changed attitude, but after a while I ended up ignoring that. I blocked out everything, and I stayed in this solitude when I was around him. I seemed to accept my fate. I became used to putting on a social mask. Continuing to socialize and go about my daily life, but only because I had to. However, the problem did not go away. It was a struggle to put on a charade everyday. I fell deeper in desolation, and started to slowly back away from friends and family, sometimes completely shutting everyone out.

This period of living with my husband was a dark time of my life. I felt like a prisoner, but one who had volunteered to be imprisoned. We drifted like two ships on different oceans for months. We were living in the same house, but we hardly spoke to one another. The feeling of entrapment seemed mutual, since we were married, we could not just bolt out of the relationship like former ones so quickly. How humiliating would that be to get a divorce after only being married for such a short time. I knew my family would be disappointed if we ended our marriage abruptly. It had only been months of living so miserably; maybe time would change things. I am not one to give up easily, so I was prepared to endure the suffering longer.

Eventually, I started to lose hope in my marriage altogether. I felt caged. Even the simplest tasks became painful. I lacked motivation. Days blended together. Heaviness filled my mind and heart, and this spilled over to my body. The emotional drain was physically exhausting me; I would sleep and nap for hours on end. Happiness became this distant abstract idea of the past. The more I tried to speak to my husband, the more of a stone wall I received. Maybe he was trying to communicate with me as well, and I was difficult to get through to. It was at a standstill of little communication for months.

I finally realized that I could not go on that way longer. Two things could either happen ... I could decide to get professional help or I might attempt something drastic like suicide. I was scared of the latter, so decided it was time to reach out for support. Not knowing where to start, I felt a deep urge to call on God for the first time in life. This was the only idea that seemed to make sense. It was the first step in a spiritual journey I had taken in life.

Little did I know, God was calling me too, and He was pursuing me just in time.

> *To him the doorkeeper opens, and the sheep hear his voice, and he calls his own sheep by name and leads them out.–John 10:3 (ESV)*

I began to feel that there was something deep inside of me, a longing to reconnect to something, but I was not sure what that "thing" was. I wanted to make things different in my marriage, and somehow correct the situation I found myself in, I needed a guide to a better path and future. I needed the Lord.

I spent many hours crying, and for the first time in my life I was praying and crying for God to save me. This was the start of a new and wonderful expedition, the road of faith. I started this journey looking for two things: God and somebody who could save my marriage. In the end, God was going to save me instead.

The first thing I did was look for a church that was right for me. As I went to different churches around Hawaii, I was searching for something, and I could not seem to find it. I left many churches without feeling any different. At some, I left in the middle of mass or service. I would leave because I felt more anxious, like something was not right. I did not belong there was all I could sense. It was disappointing that the spiritual connection I was desperate for was not happening.

Then one day, a fateful divine appointment happened. I met two wonderful ladies that invited me to their church. This simple act changed the course of my life. They had a polite way of inviting me, and this made me feel as if they really cared about me, but were not pressuring me in any way. It was a new and refreshing feeling of warmness that came from these women. I agreed to visit their church. It was God's perfect timing. I am so thankful to these godly women who are still a part of my life today. Their simple act of obedience to God's prompting in their heart in inviting me to their small family church on the other side of the island from me, was the flint that would start the journey of transforming my life forever.

It was at this church, The Wave Christian Fellowship, that something happened. As the opening worship band was playing and the church was singing along, I had an encounter with Jesus.

The worship music played and the pastor preached, and tears streamed down my face, but for the first time they were not sad, depressive tears. They were something different. When I left that Sunday, I left with a sense of peace that I had not felt in months. I felt a lightness. I was happy and hopeful about my life even though the circumstances of my marriage seemed to be getting worse. The tribulation with my husband was painful, but I was experiencing peace and joy at the same time, and now I know that was a gift from the Lord. I was hanging on in that dark valley, Jesus was starting to answer my prayer, bit by bit. There was still a light inside of me, even if it was just a faint flicker.

Lord, even when your path takes me through the
valley of deepest darkness, fear will never conquer

*me, for you already have! You remain close to me
and lead me through it all the way. Psalms 23:4
(Passion Translation)*

We tried couple's counseling, but it was not successful. He would complain about trivial things. He would say, "She doesn't let me hang out in my underwear all day and watch TV. She always wants to go and do things. I am tired, I work a lot, sometimes I just want to be home." Our personality conflict and different values in life were evident in these counseling sessions. Yet they were little, trivial, shallow complaints, with no solution ever proposed or discussed. After attending counseling for a couple months, I suspected that our marriage was on the brink of failure. Something was eating my husband up inside, and he would not speak to me about it. There was no comfort left for me in the house we shared.

The counselor suggested we take a trip together and get away. A last-ditch effort to resuscitate this marriage in the shadow of death. We went to the Big Island of Hawaii to explore Volcano National Park and other sights on that magical isle. It was a beautiful four days together exploring and connecting like we had in the beginning of our relationship. Unfortunately, this trip could not save our marriage. It was a great time and glimpses of happy times in the past surfaced. However, as soon as we returned home, things went back to cold silence, distance, and basically being roommates again.

After a few weeks of attending The Wave Christian Fellowship, I began to feel as if this new church was my home. For the first time in my life I felt at home in church. I was welcomed with genuine kindness as soon as I entered this church that meets in a public-school cafeteria by the sweet women of the church. The people made me feel like family. They embraced me with warm hugs, called me by my name and asked questions to get to know more about me. Most importantly, I felt God's presence in this small church. A feeling that is just indescribable. A feeling that once you have it, you could never live without it again. A love so overwhelming that no matter any circumstance happening, comfort and peace overtake your soul. It is supernatural, because anyone who could see the state of my marriage would never understand the peace, love, and joy I could feel during this time with God. This encounter with God started a lifelong renewing in my mind, heart, soul and spirit. All I knew at the time was that I did not want to live without God's presence any longer. As I started to connect with God, something kept reminding me that this happiness would be short-lived. A feeling inside me kept telling me something bad was about to happen.

A month after our inter-island excursion to Big Island, I had an urge to take a pregnancy test. As I took the test, I remember feeling nauseous and anxious, like could this be real; we were only intimate for four days in Volcano National Park, in the past six months; there was no way I could really be pregnant.

Lo and behold, a real miracle…it was positive. I was pregnant.

Of course, as I write this, I am so thankful for that miracle. I love my son more than anyone on the planet, but I have to be honest. When I saw positive, I cried, and these were not joyful tears. I was scared and afraid to tell my husband. I was in shock. How could this be? I felt like a trapped bird in her cage again. The tunnel of darkness was getting larger right as I was starting to find my way out. I did not know what to do next. I quickly started sinking back into the abyss of depression that I had been desperately trying to pull myself out of.

My husband and I had not spoken in weeks. We had not even shared the same room for more than a few minutes. We avoided each other, but I had to find the strength within myself to speak to him about this new life that was now inside of me, this new life that was also his.

When I finally gathered the courage to tell my husband, I sent him a text that said, "We need to talk." My husband texted me and let me know he wanted to talk as well.

I waited anxiously at home. When he returned from work, I said, "You first."

At first, he struggled to find words, and he tried to make himself comfortable. Finally he said, "I want a divorce."

Almost simultaneously I said, "I am pregnant."

The room suddenly felt filled with death, as if the light bulbs in the room had burned out. A breeze blew through an open window, a hard reality had just arrived into our lives. I was not sure how much I was to blame or he was to blame. Who was the villain? Who was the victim? Maybe there was not a villain or victim. Maybe we were just two lost people that jumped into marriage without real thought or counsel. My husband and I sat and stared at one another, both of us looking as if we had seen a ghost.

For the next few weeks, my husband and I finally found something that we had in common again. We were praying for the same thing, praying that we would go to the doctor's appointment and they would tell us the test was a false positive, and we could go on with our divorce and move on with our lives. If I had not been pregnant, we would have just divorced and moved on and it would have ended this painful chapter of my life.

However, God had other plans. He was way ahead of us with *His* planning. As we got to the military hospital for the first doctor's appointment, I felt a great deal of anxiety. It was nearly crippling. The waiting room felt like a factory sterile and large. There were countless pregnant women sitting in the waiting room. I was just another number going back to a random doctor. I sat there, thinking to myself, *how many of these women are happy?* And while most seemed happy, I could only imagine the worst for them. Bitterness and resentment were taking ground in my heart.

My blood was drawn, and the doctor confirmed my fears...I was definitely pregnant. There was a life growing inside of me. Then the doctor performed my first ultrasound and informed me that I was eight weeks pregnant. For the first time we saw the little nugget of life. It was a beautiful miracle in the midst of a storm.

The doctor stopped as she was moving the ultrasound device across my belly. She kept coming back to the same spot on my belly and stopping again. On the screen, I saw something else growing near the fetus. It was a small round mass, about the same size of the fetus. The doctor moved the ultra sound device away and then came back to it again. She looked concerned, as if she was analyzing this other growth inside of me. Was it another baby? Was I having twins? The doctor enlarged the mass of the tissue on the screen.

Then she turned to me and said, "I'm sorry to tell you this, but you also have a tumor inside of your uterus. The baby and this growth will be fighting for the same space."

Without any compassion or emotion in her voice, the young doctor informed me of all the risks now involved with my pregnancy. I had previous surgeries to remove other fibroid tumors similar to the one forming now. Twice in my twenties these masses formed and wreaked havoc on my body. The first one was extreme. I was very young and naïve and ignored all the extreme menstrual cycles. I ended up in the emergency room having four blood transfusions followed by a surgery to remove the mass. The doctor explained that I would have a high-risk pregnancy and that there was a high probability that my baby would be removed at 34 weeks to avoid the rupture of my uterus. The risk of a contraction was too high for my body. If my uterus ruptured, the baby and I could likely die. This news was overwhelming. It was too much information for me to take in. It was all happening too fast and then the young doctor's eyes lit up. She seemed to be excited about the opportunity to be my doctor and to perform this C-section early, which made me feel like a science experiment that would bring glory to her budding career instead of a human.

My husband and I walked out of the appointment. We did not speak to one another. Again, we looked like we had seen ghosts. I remember saying to God, *I can't take another thing. This really is all I have in me.*

As we drove back home, the fear inside me left me emotionally numb. I felt nothing, almost like I had died. At this point, I wasn't angry. I was disappointed in almost everything. I knew God existed, but so early in my walk of faith I just did not understand. How could a God that loves me let this happen to me? I did not understand that being a Christian did not mean there were no suffering and heartbreak. Did God love me? Where was He? I had started attending church, praying and getting to know who Jesus was. Did this mean the pain would stop? Was this baby going to die? Would my uterus rupture and kill us both? And what about my soon to be ex-husband? Where did he fit in this picture? The questions were unending and left my head spinning.

My husband remained quiet, but I knew his mind had to be racing. How could it not be with the devastating news we were given?

As soon as we got home, my husband decided it was the time to finally come clean, as if this was the right moment to clear his conscience. When we arrived at our house, he told me about his indiscretions in our marriage. The guilt had become too much for him to bear.

After this confession, I experienced a true fit of rage. Something I had no control over at the time. I exploded for the first time in my life. All this time of pain, guilt and questioning what happened to my marriage was coming out, and it came out all at once in a violent, extreme way. A lot of property was damaged, a red suitcase was packed, and I was on my way back to Florida to be with my family within a couple of days.

Chapter 4

Where Are You, God?

———

Not by might, nor by power,
but by my Spirit, says the LORD of hosts.
- Zechariah 4:6 (ESV)

I was on my way to my parents in Jacksonville, Florida and could only feel the heartbreak and fear grow by the second. Leaving my husband behind to survive this pregnancy was the first action I took. A new chapter of my life to face. I could start afresh, possibly one day. But first I had to survive this pregnancy, and it was going to take time, as well as God's strength and spirit, and lots of it. A trust in God to win my battle would have to be built. Like when David faced Goliath, he had to completely rely on God's strength to win the battle. His promise to defeat the giant was not proud boasting, but sincere trust in God—something that at the time I could not even comprehend, since I was operating in survival mode.

When I arrived at my parents' house, I appeared to be a totally different person. The depression, pain, fear, and anger had taken hold of the daughter they raised and changed her into a shell of a person. I would lay in bed for days weeping. It took tremendous physical strength to even walk to the bathroom. My mom would bring me food and drinks, and even consuming them was a strain. Victorious days consisted of days where I could muster the energy to eat at the dining room. What remained was a broken human with an innocent life inside of her fighting for a chance. My parents took me in and cared for me, probably better than any partner could. The first and biggest blessing God gave me during this season was my mom and dad. My first month or so in Jacksonville I rarely left the house. In fact, some days getting out of bed and walking to the kitchen meant victory. Depression was winning and the farther I sank into it, the more paralyzed and lost the real Raiza was. By now, suicide was a thought I would contemplate again and again. I was done with all the suffering, I had had enough, it was just too painful. The enemy was controlling my mind.

> *The thief comes only to steal and kill and destroy;*
> *I have come that they may have life and have it to*
> *the full. John 10:10 (ESV)*

The thoughts I would hear in the long, restless nights were *"this pregnancy is going to kill us anyway, just stop the suffering now. Or just keep this baby from the pain of being a statistic and your parents from having to take care of us forever. End it now and everyone can move on."*

I even devised a plan of how I was going to end my life. My parents live on the river in Jacksonville, near bridges to the downtown area. When my parents were sleeping, I would take my mom's car and drive it off the bridge. This is the black plan the enemy had created in my mind, and I was ready to execute it.

My incredible parents understood that I was in a deep stage of grief and gave me space while making sure I was eating and was safe and as comfortable as they could make me. I had expected them to pressure me into doing things and going out in public. I had expected them to knock on my door a dozen times a day, to check up on me, but they did not. I appreciated that. They let me be me. They let me grieve. But just like all things, this grieving and sobbing had to come to an end. My parents were the first to recognize this and helped me start climbing out of the darkness. They wanted the Raiza they knew and loved to return; they wanted their daughter back. The problem was, that even I did not recognize myself anymore, and I did not know where Raiza was. After all the suffering and trauma, my identity became a broken, soon-to-be-divorced woman, with a high-risk pregnancy who maybe would not survive the next seven months. Fear and depression were winning.

Finally, one morning, my dad had seen enough of this. He forced me to go to breakfast with him. Up to this point, my parents had let me just sulk and grieve and wallow in my sadness, but not anymore. When my dad asked me to join him for breakfast, I said yes because I had by now realized that this life of perpetual lamenting was not only affecting me but also others around me. The conversation my dad and I had during breakfast is one I will never forget. Almost instantly as we started having breakfast my dad spoke and said, "I don't know where my daughter went, but your mom and I are here. We are going to help you get better, but it is time you start doing the work to get better. You must do this because life is not about you anymore, you have my first grandchild inside of you and it is time to get well for this baby." This hit me harder than anything before. My father's words were heavier than any of the sufferings I had faced. I could finally feel again. The sense of coming back to reality was snapping back into me. I felt guilty for the pain I was causing my parents and the little life inside of me fighting. Almost instinctively I said *OK*. This conversation was the first glimmer of hope in this excruciating chapter of life. I knew my parents would be by my side every step of the way for me and my unborn baby.

This was the beginning of my dad protecting my son. At the time, we did not even know the sex of the baby, yet he was already in love with being a grandfather. I decided to get professional help, and within the week, I was in therapy with Dr. D. This man who sits on a bouncy yoga ball while he talks to patients is a gift. I spent many hours just crying on his comfy couch. As hard as it was to sit and talk about the things that had transpired, and where I was emotionally at the time, he would listen and give me an ounce of hope with every visit.

During those torturous moments of darkness, at night I would turn Pandora on to Jesus Culture music. This worship band was something shared with me by my soon-to-be ex-mother-in-law. She told me about a band name Jesus Culture that she would listen to during a really hard time in her life. She too had been through a lot, and I could sense some connectivity between our stories and followed her lead to give the music a chance. There was something about this music, a divine peace that would ease the pain at night and helped me rest. In the darkest moments, when I was serious about taking my life, supernatural strength would lead me to listen to this music and it was as if God was speaking to me. *"Hang on daughter, I will give you comfort, rest in me."* I was taking steps forwards. I was getting better. Today, Jesus Culture music continues to be a regular spiritual tool for me to help me find peace and joy in the midst of life's chaotic moments and tribulations. Even when life seems to be going my way and opportunities abound, Jesus Culture music brings me to the presence of God, where so many beautiful things ensue. In the fearful darkness of those nights in pregnancy, this music would ease my soul.

A high-risk pregnancy is a terrifying experience. As my baby grew, so did the tumor inside. The fight was on for that fetus to not be too cramped and have health complications, and also for my uterus to not get so big that it would rupture from prior scars and surgeries. At the 13-week appointment, both of my parents were present. Without even knowing we would find out the sex of the baby, we saw his legs wide open and knew it was a boy! The elation on my dad's face was priceless. The first boy to join our family. It was such a joyous moment in the middle of hell. A memory that lives so close to my heart. Those that know my dad, know that great big smile and cackle he makes when he is so excited about something. I had never seen my father as ecstatic about anything more than the boy he waited thirty years to have in our family.

Meanwhile, I had not heard from my husband, and as heart-breaking as that was, I kept making my doctor appointments and therapy appointments, and I started attending a megachurch in Jacksonville called Celebration Church that my mom's dear friend Margaret brought me to. During the praise and worship, the same thing occurred that would happen at my church in Hawaii. The tears that streamed down my face onto my growing belly were not the sad and full-of-despair tears. These tears were beautiful; it was time with God and I felt Him close to me, strengthening me to make it through another day. It was something that I looked forward to all week long—that touch from God.

At twenty weeks of pregnancy, my anxiety was high. I was preparing for the biggest ultrasound where they would be checking on the tumor and scanning all of the vitals and organs of my baby. I went to church the day before the appointment and that is when I heard God speak to me for the first time in my life. It is a difficult experience to describe when God speaks. A still, small voice that was so powerful, it struck my heart, mind, soul, and spirit simultaneously. I heard God say.... *Let me take this from you.* At that moment in praise and worship I fully surrendered my heart to Jesus and knew that my baby and I would be okay. We would be fine. We were in God's hands. My heart was fully convicted in this. I finally felt peace, joy, and comfort in the midst of all my negative circumstances. Margaret, who is a spiritual mentor to me today, came over to pray for me and my baby that same evening. As she prayed, tears rolled down my large pregnant belly and my heart was at rest.

> *And the peace of God, which surpasses all understanding, will guard your hearts and your minds in Christ Jesus. Philippians 4:7 (ESV)*

Margaret is an anointed intercessor. A prayer warrior to countless people in her life in ministry. Many that have prayed with her, myself included, say she has a direct line to God. I went to bed with a different prayer that evening for the first time. I knew Jesus answered my prayer for a healthy baby boy, now I was praying for a joyful baby, for the Lord to shield this boy from all the pain and sadness in my heart. For I had endured all of it for him. That evening was the first night in my pregnancy I went to bed with a sound mind and rested a full night's sleep.

The next morning, I went to my doctor's appointment with that same sense of peace still flowing. I already knew my baby's scan of vitals would be normal and that he was developing healthy and fine. The nurse who had been monitoring my uterus at the high-risk clinic had me all set and began the ultrasound. We immediately saw my baby moving around, but something was missing. The tumor that had been growing alongside of my son up unto the week before, was gone. At first, I could sense the nurse shocked and in denial. I just knew deep down that a miracle from God happened.

How could this be? The nurse called the doctor in who also spent time searching for the fibroid tumor and to his surprise he confirmed, it had vanished. Of course, the medical staff concluded that the hormones that week had done something drastic, and that was the reasoning for the disappearance of the tumor, but I knew that was my great healer, Jesus Christ. My Savior coming through in His miraculous way. The extensive scans of my son's organs and body concluded a perfectly healthy baby growing. The risk of rupture from contractions do to prior surgeries was still relevant, but I was not fearful. God's protection was on us. I might have danced my way out of that appointment that day, a glimpse of the old Raiza coming back.

At twenty weeks of pregnancy, I was experiencing moments of joy. Determined to kick the depression, I kept working with God to climb myself to victory over this mountain. Counseling sessions were working, I was needing less sessions a week as the pregnancy progressed. I felt stronger and more encouraged daily.

I made two new friends, the only friends I had during my pregnancy in Jacksonville. Sara was also pregnant with a boy. I met her though a mutual friend. It was wonderful to have a friend to walk through pregnancy with. She was funny, smart, and kind, and her husband was great too. They still remain such a special family in my life. Ellsie was also new to Jacksonville and a mutual friend introduced us as well. She was looking for a nursing job, and I introduced her to my dad to help her on that pursuit. Ellsie and I instantly clicked on many levels. Her bright light and caring heart are undeniable. I was so thankful to God to bring these two women in my life as support systems in my hardest hour. I learned then this is often a way that God works; when we are hurting and in such dire circumstances, he hears our prayers and answers in the form of people. I just needed my eyes and heart open to them and willing to make the connection.

My lifelong friends from my hometown of Pensacola were also a source of tremendous support to me, as well as the few friends from Hawaii that would call and check on me throughout my pregnancy. My two best friends, Emilie and Melissa, hosted the most beautiful and special baby shower in Pensacola. Every detail was perfect. My friends went above and beyond to create the most memorable shower I could imagine. The overwhelming love I felt that day was another gift from God to show me how even though our circumstance of being a single-mom home was not ideal, we were loved and cherished by many. God was showing me; I could walk this journey out and I was supported.

At eight months pregnant, I heard from my estranged husband. This was his child as much as it was mine. It was difficult to speak to him. I personally did not want anything to do with him, but I knew that was not God's will. My husband wanted me to know that his sister was getting married and he would be coming to Florida.

He suggested I go with him to the wedding. It did not seem like he sincerely wanted me there, and against my therapist and parent's advice I agreed to go. Not for my sake, but for my child's. I wanted him to know his father.

He came in town and needless to say, it was an extremely awkward and hard time. All the weeping and crying that had ceased came back like a flood during that visit. I had been holding on to a dream for my son. All the outside world chatter of him being a "statistic" coming from a broken home and having a single mother had been weighing so heavy on my heart. I was willing to sacrifice my own life and heart just be with this man who I knew did not love me and I did not love, all so that my son would not come from a broken home. It was complete confusion in my heart.

The Lord had a different plan; a much better plan for me and my son. During that visit at my sister-in-law's wedding, God spoke to me, again. He released me from my marriage and told me that this marriage was not His plan for me. Those words from God were exactly what I needed to hear. I had been hanging on to faith that God would do a miracle and somehow heal our relationship. With this closure, and assurance it was just not God's will to see our marriage reconciled, I changed my prayer to ask for the Lord's guidance in being two loving parents. I began to pray for him to be a great father and that the Lord would heal our hearts to be loving co-parents to our son one day. I held on to the belief that just because a child comes from a broken home, the child did not have to be broken. I put my hope in Jesus to give me wisdom to maintain a joyful and peaceful childhood for my son, to get us to that place where that would be the norm.

Chapter 5

Just Keep Walking...

Remember not the former things, nor consider
the things of old. Behold, I am doing a new thing;
now it springs for, do you not perceive it?
I will make a way in the wilderness
and rivers in the desert.
Isaiah 43:18-19 (ESV)

My last month of pregnancy was physically miserable. I gained 60 pounds and was in physical therapy for excruciating back pain that made me unable to sit for longer than 10 minutes increments. My giant watermelon belly caused the ribs in my back to shift, and the only way I could get comfortable was to lie down or stand bent over. However, even though I was in so much physical pain, my spirit was getting better day by day. By the end of my pregnancy, I was going to counseling just one or two times a week, and I was even laughing and joking with Dr. D in sessions. I continued making new friends while living in Jacksonville, and I started to connect with other people in my life again.

I ended up finding a different church from my mentor. The pastor of that church started a marriage series on the Book of Solomon and it was just too painful for me to attend. Hearing sermons on what a godly marriage should look like brought overwhelming sadness to my fragile state. Another friend invited me to her new church. It met in an old Walmart and was small at the time. (It is an extraordinarily large megachurch now, ranked among the fastest growing churches in America today.) I learned and grew in my faith every week while attending The Church of Eleven 22. Often, I would go to multiple services a weekend. My heart longed for those praise and worship times when the presence of God was shining down on me. This time was precious during such a trying period of my life. It was an overwhelming comfort and love that would fill me at these services. I would gain strength to continue moving forward to the next week.

Because of the high-risk status of my pregnancy, at 35 weeks the doctors ordered amniocentesis to test the amniotic fluid. This fluid determines the development of the lungs in the baby. The final major organ to develop and the sign to operate to take the baby out without a dangerous contraction. This involved a giant straw-like needle going into my belly to test the fluid. The first time I saw the needle I wanted to faint, but it turned out to be the least of the pain or fear I experienced in the weeks and months before these tests. I went in to have this test done three times. The third time was the charm, my son's lungs were ready to be out in the world. I was beyond ready to deliver this baby, and to have my child outside of my body.

During this time, I spent a lot of time listening to Jesus Culture worship music and praying. The supernatural, divine peace of the Lord kept me in positive spirits during these anxiety-ridden days. I knew Jesus was walking with me in lockstep in this tribulation. My baby and I were protected by the King of Kings, so nothing could go wrong. The Lord gave me that assurance, and I was at peace with my pregnancy. I chose to trust in God's promise that He was in control and we would survive this pregnancy. All of the risks involving the delivery faded away. I was relieved of all my fears of my uterus rupturing and killing myself and my baby. I had to focus on my faith in Christ and ride it out.

At Week 38, my C-section was finally scheduled. My son was to be born on December 20, 2012. I let his father know the date, and he arrived in town on December 19. It was an awkward evening having him with me in these final hours of pregnancy all of a sudden, and staying in the guest room at my parents' house. I could sense he was anxious about the scenario as well, but I was thankful he was there to witness the birth of his son.

We woke up at six in the morning and headed to the hospital to meet our son. I had heard many horrifying stories about C-sections, but fortunately mine was not traumatic. In fact, it was the easiest part of my pregnancy. I remember lying down with the screen over my belly and seeing my legs in the air for a brief moment. I thought, *"Okay, I did not lift my legs and I cannot feel them, so this medicine definitely works."*

I could not see anything behind the screen that was set up between me and my baby. My son's father was in the operating room with me. Within a few minutes our son was out and his dad was able to see him. He was not breathing normally, so he was rushed to the Neonatal Intensive Care Unit (NICU) before I could see him.

I looked at my son's father, and he looked like he was going to pass out. "I have never seen so much blood," was all he could say.

A couple of hours later, I laid eyes on my son for the first time in the recovery room. His breathing was normal and they brought him out of the NICU. He was 9 pounds, 6 ounces, 19 inches long, and he had a full head of dark hair. He was given the nickname "toddler-man baby" in the NICU. The nurses gave him this nickname because of his full head of hair, large size, and beautiful features. He was, and still is, the most perfect sight I have ever seen. Meeting my son, James, erased any fear, pain, or depression I had walked through for the past year-and-a-half. I would do everything I walked through a million times over for this precious baby in my arms. This tiny human was a true miracle of joy, love, redemption and God's grace. Many prayers were answered in one little body.

His father and I stayed in the hospital. We only had a few hours of sleep, but just like so many new parents, we, and all of our family, were so madly in love with our son that we managed to stay awake. Even though Tim and I were not together as a loving married couple, we were together as new parents.

We left the hospital on Christmas Eve with our perfect little Christmas present. Tim stayed a few more days before heading back to Hawaii. The days that followed were a sweet time where I soaked in being still, taking in every part of this new life, and walking around like a sleepless zombie. I knew James' dad was heartbroken to leave his son behind, and I was sad for him.

When James was eleven days old, I started to get in the hang of breastfeeding, and it was our first New Year's Eve together. My parents were scheduled to go to a party, but my dad made the fateful decision to stay home with us and my grandmother Nena instead. Around 8 that evening, I was feeding my son and felt that something was not normal. He went limp in my hands. As I looked down at him, he was white as a ghost. I lifted him up. I saw his complexion turn blue and purple. My baby was not breathing. I screamed for help and within seconds both of my parents were in the room. The next couple of minutes were a blur, but 911 was called, and my dad ran through the house with my lifeless baby in his hands toward the car.

I remember screaming at my father to put the baby on the ground and give him CPR. My father laid James on the floor near the doorway to the garage, and began to breathe for him. I prayed and cried, and by the time the emergency responders arrived, my son was breathing on his own again. My dad saved my son's life. We climbed into the ambulance and took our first ride together to the hospital. That New Year's was spent in the ER going through countless tests and then being admitted for the weekend, to monitor and determine what happened. I did not leave my baby's side. I did not even want to walk down the hall to the vending machines to get a snack and leave him in the room alone. We spent 72 hours in the hospital.

The cries from the babies that did not have family and parents with them broke my heart the entire time. I had an entirely new appreciation for the nurses who worked in that wing of the children's hospital. They were not only nurses; they were family to the babies that did not have any other family there. After all the tests and examinations came back, the doctors concluded that my son was perfectly healthy. He just needed to continue to work on eating, swallowing, and breathing at the same time. He had choked while trying to feed. Nevertheless, I was traumatized and from that moment on I chose not to breastfeed. Instead, I decided to be a human cow and pump milk for my child for the next four months of his life.

As soon as the doctor cleared me for exercise, I was moving and active. I was ready to get back in shape physically and mentally. I was also ready to figure out what my new life with my son would look like. I began attending a strength and conditioning workout class at a gym where my dad trained judo. It is an MMA gym in Atlantic Beach. I was still seeing my therapist, but only about once a week at this point. I filed for divorce, hired an attorney and thought, *"Okay, this should be easy. Life will move on quickly from here."* Unfortunately, that was not the case. Divorce was an ugly experience. I was given some hope with the peaceful birth of our son and my own healing; yet, moving forward with life as a single mom and all of the legalities involved with divorce, custody, and child support, were another story and storm to fight through. Again, I knew I needed God to hold my hand throughout the entire experience.

There were probably different reasons our divorce quickly became a telenovela (a Spanish soap opera). I became very angry, mostly at men in general. It disgusted me to hire attorneys and spend so much money on something that I thought could and should be so simple. My attorney's office was right down the street from my new MMA gym. I often scheduled appointments with my attorney before a workout class, and then I would go work out so hard to try and release all the anger built up in me from the hour before. I soon started watching the jiujitsu classes right after the workout and noticed there was only one female, and she was small but mighty—like a real-life ninja.

The owner of the training gym, Darren, encouraged me to try jiujitsu since I had been doing the strength and conditioning and Muay Thai classes regularly. Darren is one of those people that just shines bright. His kindness, compassion, and high energy could motivate anyone, even an angry woman like me at that time. That gym space became my second home. Outside of my dad, Darren was the first healthy relationship I had experience with a man in a couple years. He still remains a wonderful coach and friend in my life when I visit Jacksonville. All the people there were very kind and inspiring athletes who pushed me toward my goals, although I was not in an emotional space to let people in.

The first time I tried jiujitsu, I talked Kate, my one girlfriend from the Muay Thai class, into joining me. At the time, the sport was so male-dominated, and I really did not like males at the time, so it was a catch-22 for me.

I did not want to be around a male. However, the thought of learning to choke one or break one's arms or legs was a selling point for me.

Kate and I definitely stuck out in that crowd. Even as the warmups began, we had no idea how to do the moves, and the men in the class were going through the moves so quickly. It was a frustrating experience for me. I had always had some athletic ability, but I was never a star at any one sport. I could play them and participate and hold my own, but this sport was completely different.

It was like my brain and body were not connected and the coordination to do the moves was not clicking. I left the gym that night feeling silly and kind of defeated. Never in my life did I think, *Well, I just can't do that*. But in that drive home, I had so many negative thoughts about participating in jiujitsu. I fell asleep that evening feeling beat up inside and out. When I returned to the gym the next morning for the strength and conditioning class, I was encouraged with Darren's enthusiasm to give jiujitsu some time to get the hang of it. He definitely helped me feel comfortable with my complete lack of coordination and ability to even do the warmup drills, let alone the technique. I am thankful for his genuineness and positivity. If it were not for his encouragement, I might have quit before even giving the sport a real chance. Darren's grace and empathy for his students is a characteristic that keeps his gym alive and thriving. He meets people where they are at physically and helps them get to their goals. I decided to commit for one month and then determine if jiujitsu was for me.

Kate was a supportive friend, and although jiujitsu was not for her, she came along with me for a couple weeks to be my partner. I wish I could say things clicked and I was starting to understand the sport, but that was not the truth. Something about not being able to do any of the moves equally frustrated and motivated me. This sport was a tangible experience of the perseverance in the spirit the Lord was giving me. I knew I would never quit following Jesus, no matter how difficult it would be. And now this incredibly challenging sport was beginning to capture my heart as well. I remember the first night Kate and I actually sparred. It was probably one of the funniest sights to witness. I am sure it was great entertainment for all the guys on the mat that evening. We had no clue what we were doing, and we were just rolling around a mat with no control for five minutes wrestling.

At the end of the month I was still completely lost in jiujitsu. Even though I was only able to do a few of the warmup drills, I was hooked and determined to decode this sport. I kept going week after week and improving bit by bit. The best part of these 60-90 minutes was that my mind was so focused on the lesson and trying to keep up with the class that I really did not have room for any other thought. These 2-3 times a week were where thoughts of my contentious divorce or my dismal situation in life never popped into my head, and these small spaces of time were helping to heal the wounds of all that had happened. Those thoughts could not enter during jiujitsu practice. This sport was a gift from the Lord to help me escape and keep some sanity during the process of my divorce. I called it my "choke-therapy time." About four months into training, I received my first stripe on my white belt. I could not believe it. At the time, it felt like the biggest accomplishment in my life.

Just like many skills, in life, there are things that come easy and natural to some, but are difficult for others. I am still in awe of people who can learn a move in one class at the dojo. For some people, submissions and moves come with such ease. Unfortunately, I am not one of those types of jiujitsu practitioners. The amount of lessons and repetition it takes me to learn any single move is embarrassing. As a special education teacher, this sport really has helped me understand my students on a deeper level. All of the times I would be yelling in my head, *"Okay kid, why don't you know this word or that 3 times 3 is 9. We have done this countless times. It is like the weekend erases your mind every time."* Now, I was that frustrating student. I went through a difficult phase of learning, but the instructors patiently guided me and taught me. Even today, I have such patient coaches that keep pouring into me as I continue to progress slowly.

Jiujitsu is an individual journey that is done in a community. People are there for different reasons and have different goals. Some want to be champions; they compete, train at full capacity to be the best, and win at tournaments. Others enjoy it for exercise and the friendship aspect at the gym, or they are there to learn self-defense and stay in shape. Whatever the reason, jiujitsu is a sport with so much complexity, both physically and mentally. As you train more, you become a human weapon and everything starts to change. A physical change takes place in your body, as you exercise and strengthen it. Changes also happen in your mind. Learning to play the game of jiujitsu and spar is like playing chess with your body. I noticed a new mind-body connection form in me that was never present before.

To me, jiujitsu also has many parallels with Christianity. We are on our own individual journey with God. Each of us has our own unique relationship with Him, but we come together as a community in church to learn, have fellowship, grow, and to praise and worship God. We grow and transform over time with our walk with God, just like we grow and transform as we continue to train jiujitsu. As we go deeper and deeper on each journey, there is no endpoint or arrival, but throughout the journey we only get better with time and perseverance.

Chapter 6

Leap of Faith

*Do you see what this means-all these pioneers
who blazed the way, all these veterans cheering
us on? It means we'd better get on with it. Strip
down, start running—and never quit!.... Keep
your eyes on Jesus, who both began and finished
this race we're in. Study how he did it because
he never lost sight of where he was headed—that
exhilarating finish in and with God—he could put
up with anything along the way.*
–Hebrews 12:1-3 MSG

For me, my son's first year of life was filled with every human emotion known to man. I was so in love that I spent some days just staring at my baby in wonder and amazement. Living with my parents and having all their support was an incredible blessing at that time. I would not need to worry about employment until my son was ten months old, and at that point, I was ready to go back to work. My mom's love of doing laundry was a great help with an infant in the house. The four of us got into a comfortable routine of life. It was as if my son was blessed with three parents at once in the house.

I was fortunate enough to be a mom, work on my self-healing through professional therapy, and grow in my Christian faith. I know the kind of support my family gave me was a gift from God to get me to a better place emotionally. I became the most physically fit in my life and learned new skills in the area of self-defense through my martial arts training. The depression, bitterness, and despair I battled with for a year-and-a-half was dissipating day by day. My joyful spirit was making a breakthrough and I was ready to battle like a warrior to keep that joy in my heart.

The dichotomy of my life was so extreme in the first fifteen months of my son's life. I was moving on personally and starting to feel a healthy rhythm and comfort as a single mom. The Lord was blessing me with a newfound strength. Yet I was simultaneously trudging through a divorce that seemed to be a black hole with more ugly, difficult obstacles surfacing from the attorneys. The relationship between my son's father and I was at a gloomy standstill. As hard as it was to keep walking, I had full faith in my Jesus. I was patiently waiting on the miracle from God in this settlement. This was just another season of endurance with God on my side.

I never had the opportunity to go back and say goodbye to friends in Hawaii or have closure there. When James was six months old, I was very happy that an old neighbor graciously offered for him and I to travel to Hawaii for six weeks for a visit. My friend was leaving for the mainland, and we would stay and housesit. I had left the island in such heartbreak and despair eighteen months earlier. A chance to go back, see friends, and say a peaceful goodbye after leaving so abruptly sounded like a healing trip.

While in Hawaii, I was hopeful that his father and I could agree and settle the divorce once and for all if we were in the same place. Unfortunately, that dream did not happen. It was just not God's timing. I was able to have a healing experience catching up with friends and reconnecting with my church, The Wave Christian Fellowship.

While there, James was dedicated in a beautiful service on Bellows Beach on the east side of Oahu by our pastors. It was a beautiful day and I was so thankful to be back with a church family that was there at my darkest hour, dedicating my son to Christ. I trained in jiujitsu and had as good of a time as possible with friends and my son that summer, despite all of the legal drama that was happening between his father and I. It was a summer where I began to really heal and start to find my way as a single mother. I did not have my parents' help and support in household responsibilities and child care like I had at home. It was a great experience of self-reliance and also a new level of gratitude for having such amazing grandparents in my son's life.

When I returned to Florida, I was ready to get back in the classroom. I was hired in a dropout prevention program for overaged high schoolers. My students had failed in multiple grades in life and were still holding on by threads to the hope of a diploma. The trauma and difficult circumstances in these students' life were heartbreaking. These were tough working conditions. I saw more fights between students in a few months than I had seen my entire career, but the students had my heart, as they always had. It was different being a teacher now that I had a son at home. Before I had my son, I could pour all sorts of extra things into my classroom and students; mostly time, energy and money. With a child at home, it was more difficult to do many of the things I did the first seven years of my career. I struggled with the balance between home and work life, as well as the divorce proceedings. There were very difficult days and weeks of feeling like I was failing at everything. Motherhood, teaching, following Christ. If I wasn't feeling like a complete failure, I would feel okay in one area of life and a complete disaster in another. It is the walk of a working single-parent from my experience.

> *And we know that all things work together for good*
> *to those who love God, to those who are the called*
> *according to His purpose.–Romans 8:28 (NKJV)*

Even though I was going through so much stress and anxiety, I knew He would use these difficult times in life for my own good. God was using all the hurt and pain of this short-lived marriage, single motherhood, and divorce to prepare me for the great plans He had for my future. God was faithful to me and fulfilled His purpose on His time, like He always does. I was determined to not allow these difficult circumstances to define my life or get me down. I had my relationship with Jesus and the right tools that He showed me in the past two years to keep my spirit and mind in a warrior's frame of mind. Jesus, jiujitsu, worship music, and my son kept things moving forward. These were gifts and spiritual tools to keep peace, joy, and harmony in my heart through the tough moments.

When my son was 14 months old, his father came in town for our divorce proceedings. I knew the potential trial would be very expensive if we could not get to an agreement that day. I prayed for a miracle before entering the room where the judge and our attorneys were waiting. As the court proceedings began, I felt supernatural peace begin to comfort me. We left that day without resolution, which was disappointing, but that evening the Lord performed a miracle. My son's father, Tim, asked me to meet him for a drink. He wanted to talk. We met at an Irish pub near my parents' house. We had not really had much of a conversation in about a year. God was up to something.

We agreed on terms for our divorce, custody, and child support on a bar napkin.

The next morning, I handed that napkin to my attorney. *"We are done. It's over!"* I said.

Within the week, documents were drafted, signed, and sealed. The divorce was settled. It was finally over. I was so grateful to Jesus, my confidant and friend who walked it out with me, keeping me as graceful as possible through this tumultuous situation. God literally took the mountain in Tim and my life that we had been facing for 14 months and moved it in just one encounter. I had been in fervent prayer for the Lord to move in Tim's heart so that we could have a conversation and not deal with attorneys and that prayer was answered. It was the first sign of hope that Tim and I would somehow one day peacefully co-parent.

The week after my son's father left, I went on my first big trip away from my son. My adventurous friend Ellsie and I headed to Peru for the trip of a lifetime. The old Raiza from my twenties with a zeal for life and travel was back. Organizing, planning, and going on this venture was thrilling, but also nerve-wracking, leaving my baby behind for two weeks. The country of Peru was beautiful beyond belief, and the five days spent hiking and camping along the Inca Trail to Machu Picchu was incredibly healing to my spirit and soul. Although I physically hurt my knee on the countless steps, the Lord was speaking to me, and a story of hope was being spoken—a story of restoration and love for me and redemption for my son's father.

During this trip, the idea of moving back to Hawaii and giving my son an opportunity to have an active dad in his life was planted in my heart. I felt it was essential to believe in God's words. I had made the bad decision of getting married by going with the flow and seeing what would happen, but ***Proverbs 3:5-6 (NIV)*** says *"Trust in the Lord with all your heart, and lean not on your own understanding; in all your ways acknowledge him, and he will make your paths straight."* The Lord was beginning to straighten our path out, in His way. He was leading me down a path to make a message from the mess I had made. A beautiful message of grace, love, mercy, and redemption.

When I returned from Peru, I talked to my son's father about James and I moving to Hawaii. Tim was excited about the idea of having our son close to him and having the opportunity to be a part of James' daily life. He offered to help with the cost of shipping my car and other belongings to Hawaii. However, even though we were thrilled to do the co-parent thing in the same place, I was afraid to share this idea with my parents. They were so in love with James, and I knew moving from Florida to Hawaii would break their heart. It was such a hard decision to make, and I needed a word from God to help me be sure that was His will for us. That meant I needed to seek wise counsel from the people who were walking with Jesus and ministering to others, and I needed to spend extra time fasting in prayer with God asking Him where He wanted us. My mom and my spiritual mentor, Margaret, who has served as a mighty prayer warrior for Christian Healing Ministries, both suggested I make a prayer appointment to hear from the Lord.

I went to Christian Healing Ministries in Jacksonville to pray. I walked into the room and they asked me about my prayer request. I told them that I needed guidance from God on a big decision about where my son and I would live. During that prayer meeting, I heard my first prophetic word from God through a person. The prayer minister told me that the Lord knew my move will be very difficult and that it would hurt people I care about very much, but it would be a blessing for my son and I. I felt God was testing my faith, testing me to trust in His plan for our life. I left that appointment knowing that this was a part of my walk with Jesus. I knew that people in our lives who really loved us might not understand this submission to God's will, and that made it incredibly hard to share with my family. I know this often happens, but God keeps His promises. As much as I knew our move to Hawaii would hurt my parents, the Lord was working behind the scenes to bring peace for us all.

For we walk by faith, not by sight.–2 Corinthians 5:7 (NKJV)

My parents did not take the news well, to say the least. They reacted with an emotional cloud of fear, stress, worry, sadness, and anger, which made me feel helpless again in life. My parents, the biggest blessings in my life, were hurting, and it was my decision that caused this pain. I had to put my full trust in God. He would get my family through this storm to victory. As hard as it was to leave my family and the life I created in Jacksonville for my son, I was walking in obedience to the Lord, and I was excited for a new season. While planning our move, the spirits of fear and worry would attack me, but the constant help from God enabled me to make decisions accordingly and to stick with Jesus.

During the preparation season, I found a house to buy near Atlantic Beach in the Jacksonville area. It was a great property, a perfect-sized house for James and I. It was a wonderful investment and something that would be good to have in case we wanted to move back to Florida. I felt it would be a good idea to own an affordable home. I could lease it while we lived in Hawaii. This house would prove to be quite the blessing years later.

I sent my resume to schools in Hawaii, and a principal from a school with an outstanding reputation on the south shore of Oahu called me immediately. It was a phone interview that I will never forget. While talking to the principal, I heard his kindness and his love for his students and faculty. He was unlike any principal I had worked for, and I prayed he would hire me. A couple days later, I was offered a position at that school as a special education teacher at Kaimuki Middle School, a school with heart. I was not sure what this meant at the time of being hired, but loved that it was part of their vision statement. I was ecstatic. The Lord was moving me to another high need area in education, but this would be a safer setting for me.

The day finally arrived when it was time to leave for Hawaii. It was heart-wrenching to say goodbye for us, but I knew the Lord had my back, and if God is for us, who can be against us? I was ready to return to Hawaii and start a new journey with my son and his father. The Lord had convicted my heart in prayer how important it was for our son to have his father as an active part of his life. Living in Florida while Tim was in Hawaii just did not make that possible. All the years spent teaching at-risk youth, there was often a common thread I noticed between them: absent fathers. I knew my son had a father that wanted to be present, who wanted to be there daily for him. It was a leap of faith and trust in God that He would keep us protected, provide the way, and continue to heal hearts and rebuild new relationships. This time I would head to Hawaii with some new important skills as a human weapon in jiujitsu, as well as spiritual tools to guide me toward God's comfort and purpose.

I went to my last therapy appointment. I remember talking and laughing with Dr. D for the last hour. At the end of our session, he said, "Raiza, you don't need me anymore."

"Yay!" I said. "I don't need you anymore."

The spirit of depression was gone. I danced my way to my car in the parking lot. The old Raiza was back, stronger than ever. Because Jesus was walking behind, in front of, and beside me. He was the lamp on my feet lighting the way.

Chapter 7

Oss

———

Because of the Lord's great love we are not
consumed, for his compassions never fail.
They are new every morning;
great is your faithfulness.
Lamentations 3:22-23 (NIV)

I arrived back in Hawaii in the summer of 2015, ready to find housing, get settled, and have my mom bring my son to his new home state a few months later. Searching for a place to live in Honolulu without a pay stub from Hawaii was stressful. Daily, I went to look at houses that were in my price range and found dozens of other applicants looking at the same properties. I prayed for a call back from landlords, but I did not hear anything for a considerable length of time. As the days turned into weeks, I was getting nervous and again finding myself reliant on God to come through with a perfect home for us. That kind of faith was easier said than done. Doubts about my decision to uproot us so far away from the life we knew and loved began to sprout in my mind. Had I made a terrible choice? Was that really God that made me feel so sure we were supposed to move back to the islands? Or did I just make a costly, impulsive decision that I really could not afford? I was staying with friends and only had a short time to get everything ready for my son's arrival.

One morning, I was scouring the housing advertisements online and a new listing suddenly appeared. Instinctively, I had to be one of the firsts to view it. The pictures looked absolutely beautiful, and it made me feel a little hopeful. I knew not to hesitate, so I immediately called and set up an appointment to see the place. It was a charming upstairs apartment of a house in a nice neighborhood with breathtaking views of Diamondhead Crater. It was also conveniently located near my work and my son's future preschool. As soon as I met the landlord, my spirit felt at ease, as if God had lined up this extraordinary apartment for us. The landlord lived downstairs with her two daughters. Her husband worked in China and came home when he could. I could not have asked for a better landlord, and her daughter turned out to be an excellent playmate for my son.

Around the same time, my sister from New York thought it was a good idea to put a dating app on my cell that involves swiping "left" or "right" to photos. It was the rage in New York City at the time. She told me stories of her friends going on up to three dates in one evening with this app. The 5 p.m. happy-hour date, the dinner date, and then the late-night at a bar date. I could not believe the dating world had come to this. It had been years since I even considered meeting a man, and this new world of instant dating and constant choices seemed frightening and overwhelming. Cynically, I gave this app a go to see if I even had what it took to date in the ever-changing modern world.

Upon a few matches and chatting conversations I agreed to meet an interesting man that was an entrepreneur. It was an enjoyable evening, but the connection I made was not with him, but it was with his business partner, who was also on a date of his own at the bar. This man was funny, smart, handsome, and into me. We were kindred spirits, and within a matter of weeks were inseparable. After a few years away from romantic relationships, I fell into one, and I fell hard. It was as if all the godly wisdom gained in the past few years from the lessons and sermons on dating vanished. I was on the same worldly path of "hook up, shack up, break up, repeat" that I had been on all through my twenties.

I reconnected with my church, The Wave Christian Fellowship. My new boyfriend was not a believer, but he said he "supported my faith." This meant he would attend church with me. He said it made him feel great to hear positive messages, but he just could not accept that Jesus was real. His intellect would stand in the way like a barrier between him and God. Also, the idea of dating and not being physically intimate was the most foolish, archaic practice he had ever heard of. It was not something he could wrap his mind around and a main reason he could never commit to being a "Christian." What I did not realize at the time was that this relationship was also a barrier for me. It was a wedge between my growth with God, as I slowly died in my sexual sin. It was a subtle death, and I was completely ignorant that it was even occurring. Many of my friends — even ones that called themselves Christians — lived with their boyfriend or girlfriend. I chose the pieces of the Word of God that suited my life, and just ignored the parts that would cause a great shift in my life, in particular the scriptures discussing sexual immorality.

I was settling in and ready to begin the search for a jiujitsu academy to call home. Fortunately, a close friend that had just moved off the island had a girlfriend named Leila that also trained jiujitsu, so she put us in touch with each other. This woman would later become one of my most close and precious sisters in Christ. Leila was also a single mom and intimately understood my situation. She was kind enough to share where she trained, and this marked the beginning of a beautiful new era of my martial arts journey. The professor was awesome, and the dojo had a laid-back atmosphere where kids could come and play on the side of the mat while adults trained at night. This was a perfect scenario for me. The owners had a young daughter, and they were expecting a second child when I met them. As I walked into the dojo for my first class after checking out a few other dojos in the area, I was sure that this was the right academy for me. It was going to be my home for that season. I felt planted at Jiu-Jitsu Islands and was excited to keep growing in this sport, and to keep connecting with other people in the martial arts world.

Jesse was the professor of the dojo, and anyone who knows Professor Jesse can attest to the large heart, love, and passion he has for the sport of jiujitsu. His slim stature is somewhat deceptive, and does not truly reflect his amazing skills on the mat. I felt welcomed in the friendly family-style atmosphere which he had created in his dojo. The ambience was inviting, and I knew my son and I were plugging into a great community. Professor Jesse has created quite the social media platform, and many legends in the grappling world have come to train on the mats in the dojo. Yet, even with big names and superstars of the sport visiting the dojo, it retains a family that makes up Jiu-Jitsu Islands as a team with heart, humility, love, and compassion.

People of all levels, abilities, professions, ages, beliefs, and backgrounds gather on those mats with one shared goal: to grow in the sport of jiujitsu and be a part of a great community. *Proverbs 27:17 (NIV) says: "As iron sharpens iron, so one person sharpens another."* This verse proved to be true in our lives as we built each other up and encouraged one another to continue in the pursuit of our goals. The parallels with walking with the Lord in the Christian community are very similar. Every walk of life comes together with one shared goal: to follow Christ and become more like Jesus as He transforms our hearts and minds. In the dojo, people from all walks of life come to practice under one unified roof. They are from different backgrounds and different socioeconomic statuses, with different reasons for trying jiujitsu.

However, when we first start, we have one thing in common—we have no idea what we are doing.

The jiujitsu culture is one of family, love, and acceptance. There are many reasons that a person keeps showing up to the mat: to get stronger physically or emotionally, to learn self-defense skills, to get mental clarity, to lose weight and exercise, or to compete are a few. Whatever the reason may be, each person forms a bond with their training partners in the dojo. It creates a place of fellowship where you can connect on a personal level and interact with people who have a common interest or even a passion. The martial arts phrase "Oss" has many different meanings, all of which describe the culture of the community. The first type of definition includes a simple greeting or acknowledging an opponent's skills. The term also conveys the idea of "persevering when pushed," a level of grit and determination that does not leave room for giving up, even in the most arduous training sessions. Oss is a verbal reminder of a "combat spirit" and advancing with a steady positive attitude, breaching one's comfort zone, and pushing physical and mental limits. It is a journey of tremendous growth.

In Hawaii, this culture of family or "Ohana" is strong since it is an island so far away, and many people like me have their families on the mainland or abroad. It is common for dojos to become a second family, and we do life together. Birthday celebrations, Thanksgiving, New Year's beach barbecues, the list goes on for all the time spent on and off the mat together. The bond created between teammates is substantial. Lifelong friends are made as we share in the pursuit of becoming better martial artists.

When I first started jiujitsu in Florida, I was clueless, but showed up regardless. At this first stage, I found myself getting submitted every thirty seconds with each sparring round. This was an incredibly humbling experience. But I was determined to persevere, and I kept showing up to the mat, learning and growing with every practice. Jiujitsu has many similarities with Christianity. Consider how we all have different backgrounds, different socioeconomic statuses, different stories that ultimately lead us to Christ. When God calls us, and we answer His call, we show up regardless of where we stand spiritually. We are unqualified and unworthy to even come to Him. We do not have it all figured out either, and we never really "figure everything out" with God, but we have this foundation, our Rock upon which we all stand, Jesus Christ. In my case, I really did not know much about the Lord when I accepted Jesus into my heart, but that is what faith is all about. Faith is a mystery and a trust in an Almighty God that he will always make a way, even when we cannot see.

Similarly, in the church, to really follow Christ and grow to be more like Jesus, it requires more than just showing up to service on Sunday. I learned that being a Christian is not just checking off a weekly list such as "I went to church," "I prayed," "I read my Bible," or "I am saved." Christianity is not limited to routine. In fact, it is a never-ending journey with Christ. There are countless valleys and peaks, and everything in-between. God creates profound experiences in His presence in a community. He calls us to plug into a church and do life together as a body of believers. This part was hard at first, to put myself out there and join the weekly bible study, serve at church, and connect with people I did not have much in common with outside the church. But I learned the invisible thread that is our rock and foundation, Jesus Christ, connects us more than anything the world has to offer.

> *But God has so composed the body, giving greater*
> *honor to the part that lacked it, that there may be*
> *no division in the body, but that the members may*
> *have the same care for one another. If one member*
> *suffers, all suffer together; if one member is hon-*
> *ored, all rejoice together. Now you are the body of*
> *Christ and individually members of it. 1 Corinthians*
> *12:25-27 (ESV)*

I grew in my faith and walked closer and closer with the Lord, which just means I could feel God's presence consistently. A sweet comfort and love were present in the routines and steps of the day, and I knew Jesus was there by my side. I was leaving behind old ways of thinking and patterns that were not healthy, and I was learning more about the character of Jesus and how I am supposed to follow Him. Even now, God's ways still remain mysterious to me at different levels. Yet it has been the most exciting adventure to embark on, and when I glance back at my life, I see how far God has brought me. The way the Lord shows up time and again when my strength has run out, when I need a miracle, or even the divine appointments that I have not prayed or asked for, He makes them happen. All of these things are so exciting and make a life worth living. It is a reminder of what the Apostle Paul said in *Philippians 4:13 (NKJV), "I can do all things through Christ who strengthens me."* We can also boldly declare this as we draw nearer to the Lord. The love of Christ equips us in life's journey, from being infants in faith when we crawled in the journey with God to having a steady path that does not waver from the truth.

I had the unique experience of starting my journey as a jiujitsu player and a Christian around the same time. It was easy to let Jesus save me. My strength was no match for my difficult circumstance. There was nothing left in me at twenty weeks of pregnancy, but when I heard God speak, it was the easiest decision of my life to accept Jesus into my heart and let him save me and my unborn child. The actual struggle that I faced was in the "making Jesus my Lord" part of Christianity. It has been a constant battle in some seasons, and then the most blissful joy and peace imaginable in other seasons. As my faith matures, these two states of being continue to clash in my mind, but I have the wisdom to understand, "Okay, this is a spiritual attack," or "Here comes that same sin that I have struggled with trying to make its way back into my life," or to recognize, "This person or relationship is pushing me away from the Lord." Now I have the tools to combat these battles before they turn into things like anxiety, depression, bitterness, loneliness, or despair.

When I feel the attack on my peace or joy, I turn to the Lord. I pray right then and there, wherever I am. Sometimes it's a long prayer where I do cry to God, or sometimes it is just a 30-second prayer where I ask Jesus to be with me, for the Holy Spirit to rebuke whatever is happening, and for God's hand of protection and peace that surpasses all understanding. I go to my Bible when I am feeling a shift in my peace. We are so blessed to live in a day where we have access to God's written Word at our fingertips 24/7. We can always look for help within His word and find comfort. There have been many occasions when I am sitting in a workout class waiting for the instructor to start and the music that is blaring offends my spirit. The vulgar words, the misogynistic message, the objectifying of women all make me feel disgusted. My peace starts to dwindle, and so I decide to get my Bible phone app out and I start reading. I may be the only person in the workout studio laying on her mat reading scripture, but that is okay, because my peace and joy that comes from the Lord is staying put.

My personal cross I have carried has been my relationships with men. It has been a bumpy road these twenty years in the dating wilderness. As hard and sometimes traumatic these relationships have been, God was always there, pulling me through the dark. I now have spiritual tools to get me through those moments. I call on my sisters in Christ, my spiritual mentors, my time on dojo mats; the wisdom and prayer covering from my sisters is priceless. It takes just one conversation, and my peace starts to make its way back into my heart and mind. Thus, the mental clarity and "refresh" I get from training jiujitsu is a gift from the Lord. Often, I train whenever I am having a problem, whether it is related to relationships, work, finances, or anything really. When I leave, I have a new outlook. An outlook with solutions rather than just seeing problems. I find myself in the moment during those 90 minutes of training to clear my head from any thoughts except jiujitsu. I am hyper-focused on the move we are learning that day or the spar I am fighting for my life in. This hyper-focus on something other than problems shifts my perspective with answers to problems once I leave the dojo.

Things were moving in such a seamless and effortless way, once I was reconnected to the powerful Christian and jiujitsu communities and fully settled in a perfect apartment. I was dating a man I really cared about. This relationship was moving at lightning speed, which looking back was not a good sign, but I was falling in love and my eyes were blind to the red flags. I was blown away at how this impossible situation came together so quickly. It was God's grace and love that kept lining things up for me. He was hearing my earnest cries and honoring all the transformation and faithfulness I had to make in this transition in life. One thing was for sure: through the bad days or good days, God combined them to eventually give me this exciting future. His promises are more real than anything I know. I just had to wait and hold on to those promises for God's perfect timing.

This is not to say there were not any difficulties in my transition from Florida back to Hawaii. The cost of living in Hawaii as a single mom and teacher was and still is out of my league, yet I believed the prophetic word spoken over me that God wanted James and I there at this time. I had to trust that the Lord would make a way with provisions and finances to make it happen.

When James arrived after I was settled, I had our little apartment all set. His dad and I had put his race-car bed together and set his room up with superhero décor. I was so excited to see him and have him in his new home. His dad was thrilled to see him as well. We moved into co-parenting with minor bumps in the road, but overall as a team. We gave our son two loving homes, where he would always be safe and protected. Jesus had healed our hearts with supernatural forgiveness. He was making something beautiful out of the mess we had created years before.

Chapter 8

Progressive Sanctification

Therefore if anyone is in Christ, the new creation
has come: the old has gone, the new is here!
–2 Corinthians 5:17 (NIV)

Our first year in Hawaii was an adjustment. There were so many wonderful things happening, but also challenging things, as well. I felt like I was constantly trying to balance on a seesaw of extremes as I was working hard to find my way as a single mom so far away from family support. Between the struggle of balancing finances to make rent and my son's problematic behavior at preschool, I was overwhelmed with fear and panic at times. As a teacher for so many years, I could not understand how my 3-year-old son could require so many behavior-related parent-teacher conferences. These meetings exhausted me. Yet there were many blessings happening simultaneously.

My job at the middle school was a dream come true. I made instantaneous friendships with co-workers, and I was blessed with such a pleasant working environment. My students could not have been sweeter and more obedient. Oftentimes while working at this school, I felt as though I had been transported to a different time and culture where it was more common to see two-parent homes and families rather than the situation I was in. Children with respect for teachers, students with a desire to learn, and teachers with commitment to their students is the norm at this school. It was all very invigorating, and it drew a renewed sense of passion for my career as an educator. The campus stands on a hill and is maintained like no other public-school campus I have seen in my career teaching in Hawaii and Florida. The outside beauty of the perfect landscaping and freshly painted buildings gives staff and students a great sense of pride to be a part of this school. It is common to see the vice-principal on a riding lawn mower making sure the recess yard is adequate for students.

There are so many emotions, hormones, and physical changes that occur during these years of puberty. School can be such a destructive place for some teens struggling with personal matters. But this school is different. The administration has built a gem of a middle school that is filled with an extraordinary atmosphere of "aloha." I have heard many different explanations of what "aloha" means and how people show it. To me, it all boils down to love, respect, and honor. The Hawaiian culture is unique in many ways, and this spirit of "aloha" is a pillar that makes this island chain such a precious treasure. The school where I was blessed to work at exemplifies this "aloha" spirit.

Working here was different from any other school I had worked at before. In the past, I had taken so much work home, and I was continually exhausted mentally, emotionally, and physically from so many problems that riddle the public-school system in our country. Lack of resources, parental support, administration support, and high-pressure demands on student performance wore me down yearly. There were rampant examples of students suffering from emotional trauma, lacking basic needs, living in poverty, having no supervision, not having enough food, and being victims of neglect and abuse. I would pour my heart and soul into these youth daily and would feel so drained by the time I got home. Worrying about missing students, hungry students, and students that I suspected were being abused took a toll on my overall health and well-being.

The winter, spring, and summer breaks were always needed to restore my soul for another school year ahead. I adored these students, and loved to be their cheerleader, but knew I could never keep up with the demands without the vacation time.

This new school was populated by respectful and studious middle schoolers that came from loving homes. There were plentiful resources; the teachers were often not bogged down by additional work to complete at the end of the work day. It was a real blessing to be a teacher from 7 to 3 and a mom the rest of the time. Unlike many years of being a teacher who would mentor, counsel, and help students after school, evenings, and weekends regularly, this student body did not have that extreme need. The two years of attempting to balance working at an at-risk school and being the mother of a baby was incredibly challenging. God was showing me favor with this job and helping me find balance as a single-working mom between teaching and motherhood.

In addition to my wonderful new job, my son's father and I were getting along well as co-parents. We had established a routine to our custody, and James was so happy having access to both of us. We missed my parents a lot and still do, but for James, having both of his parents as an active part of his life is a priceless gift— one he certainly deserves.

Just because our family was broken, we did not have to have a broken child.

James is proof of this, as he still spreads laughter and joy everywhere.

Parent-teacher conferences at the age of three were challenging. After so many years teaching, I never thought my kid would be the "class clown." Yet, here we were as parents working through the behavior challenges that come with such a "big" personality in the classroom. We began to work as a unit as parents, with a shared goal to raise a godly man who is kind, hard-working, compassionate, and follows Christ. It is a team effort, even if we live in different homes. His father may not be on fire for Jesus like I am, but we do talk about how important our son's spiritual life is, and he respects and honors the seeds of faith that I am planting in our son. Supernatural forgiveness and healing began in this time between Tim and I. We really had to let go of the past and start a new relationship as parents. This year was a building of that.

At the same time, I was navigating the dating world as a single mom, which was a brand-new experience. My boyfriend swept me off my feet quickly. It was a whirlwind romance. We were this instant family, him, James, and I. There were dates, plenty of time together, social media PDA. Things became serious quickly when we moved in together without much thought or discussion. Looking back, this step was taken without any prayer to God. We loved one another, and he was wonderful with my son. Everything about our relationship was easy and exciting. Everything except my faith as a Christian. Again, as much as I loved God and was a believer in Jesus, making Christ my Lord in all areas was a struggle. I fell into temptation, and began living with my boyfriend. This was a true sign of me being the master of my own life and not allowing God to take charge. Living in sexual sin, even in a committed boyfriend/girlfriend relationship, has consequences. As this relationship progressed, it was clear that we were heading down two different paths. God's call on my life had me digging deeper with my relationship with Jesus, and although my boyfriend kept supporting my faith, he could not understand it for himself.

Recently, a mentor told me that one of the greatest attacks from the enemy on a godly woman is the wrong relationship with a man. I loved my boyfriend and the fun we had together, but the Lord revealed a lot to me about the relationship. When I would pray and ask God what to do, I would hear, "let him go," in that still small voice. Yet, I did not obey. For months, I held on to this relationship that was driving a wedge between Jesus and I. I kept praying for God to save him so that we could honor the Lord and get married.

The problem with this prayer was that it was not God's will. He had already told me twice, "let him go," and I did not obey. For months, I kept asking God what to do, and I heard silence.

Looking back at this time that was riddled with "drama" in the form of anxiety, jealous rage, and sadness from this relationship that turned toxic quickly, I can see exactly where I went wrong. When the Lord tells us something, He means it. It is not as if God will tell you something like, "let him go," and then you can pray for months or even years and God will change His mind. God loves me so much that He told me what to do because He was leading me away from temptation and a destructive heartbreak. I can see now, years after this time, that God just had better plans for me than that relationship because He is a loving father.

With a heavy heart, I had to end the relationship and walk away from my boyfriend because I recognized the will of God. The Lord showed me how valuable I am to Him, and that if I were to be with a man, he would have to love, cherish, and honor me at all times—something that was not the case in this relationship. My boyfriend loved and cherished me when we were in one another's presence. But when I was not around, there were other interesting women in the picture. What God has for me is that I am not to be someone's number one—rather someone's *only* one; a chosen one. The Lord's desire for me is to be with a godly man who follows Christ and is grounded in the Word of God. Someone who will lead and is centered on Christ. The struggle to deepen my relationship with Jesus and be in a romantic relationship with a nonbeliever was like two incredibly strong forces yanking at my heart simultaneously. I had made my boyfriend an idol, and God wanted to come first in my life.

> *Do not be yoked together with unbelievers. For what*
> *do righteousness and wickedness have in common?*
> *Or what fellowship can light have with darkness?*
> *- 2 Corinthians 6:14 (NIV)*

Fortunately, Christ's power and forgiveness are unmatched. The relationship with my boyfriend was built on the loose sands of emotions, physical attraction, and chemistry. And so, without the strong foundation of Christ centering both of us, the relationship crumbled.

The breakup was devastating. It was messy. It was a double broken heart for me as a mother, since I saw my son really hurt and miss him as well. And it was a tough lesson to learn, but moving forward in the wilderness of dating, I gained discernment and wisdom to not only guard and protect my heart in the future, but my son's as well. His life was attached to mine, so I had to take every step keeping in consideration that whatever I did would impact him just as much. The chains of simply going-with-the-flow dating (hook up, shack up, break up, and repeat) still had a hold on me in this relationship, and it was something I really needed God to transform in me. I needed Him to free me from this cycle for my sake and for the sake of my son.

The anxiety, despair, fear, and overwhelming sadness during this breakup was excruciating, almost worse than my divorce. We stayed in communication for a while, and it turned into a nightmare of unnecessary drama. His womanizing ways were brought to the surface, along with his idolization of money. Here I was again, in the same sinking ship God had rescued me from before, but feeling so much worse. The repercussions of my anxiety were affecting every area of my life. I had a hard time keeping up with my teaching responsibilities and maintaining my household, and the worst part was that I felt as if I was not being a good mom to my son. It was hard to be present with my son while dealing with heartbreak and anxiety.

> *For if, after they have escaped the pollutions of the world through the knowledge of the Lord and Savior Jesus Christ, they are again entangled in them and overcome, the latter end is worse for them than the beginning.–2 Peter 2:20 (NIV)*

I was experiencing this in my own life. God had brought me out of the sin before, and I stepped into the trouble once again. This time the pain was worse. I needed the year to end, to put this season behind me. When Jesus says in the Gospel of John, "I am the truth and the way," He means it. He is the way, the journey from beginning to end, and every step in between. I surrendered my heart to Jesus years before, and His love and comfort would walk this new pain out with me as well. Just because I had made a bad decision to be in this relationship and not honor God or myself, Jesus was still there. He would comfort me through the heartbreak and bring life back into my soul.

We made it through the holiday season and it was 2017, a new year. I was determined to get my joy and peace back, and not let the ways of the world steal it from me again. My church was starting a *Year in the Bible Discipleship Study*. I sat in church and listened to an announcement about our church reading through the Bible together in a year. The Holy Spirit was speaking to me *"Yes, this is the answer to your pain and anxiety, renew your mind and heart in my Word."* I made the commitment that I would read through the entire Bible for the first time in my life that year. As soon as I said yes to this, the chains of anxiety began to break. It was an immediate relief, and it came from saying yes to God. At the time I had no idea how transformational this "YES" to the Lord would be, but I was hopeful and excited that God would do something new and awesome in my life.

Chapter 9

Me Too

But seek first his kingdom and his righteousness,
and all these things will be given to you as well.
–Matthew 6:33 (NIV)

When I was eighteen years-old, my mom gave me a Bible as a gift to take along with me to college. It was a New International Version Bible. She had even taken the time to mark the books with labels for me to use. That Bible lived on my nightstand collecting dust, holding drinks and other books for many years through all of the different houses I resided in through my twenties and early thirties. I never took the time to actually read through it and seek to understand it. Every time I would try, it did not make sense to me, and I would either fall asleep or return it to the nightstand to collect dust again.

That Bible was there in my twenties, when I had a couple of scary encounters with men. I remember that there was a stranger that had been coming into my house when I lived in Miami, and he would do weird things. In one instance, someone opened my bedroom door at 4:45 a.m. I called out my roommates' names to no response, just the sounds of deep breaths. I grabbed my Bible. I lay in bed paralyzed with fear. Eventually, the footsteps went back towards the kitchen. It took the dawn breaking through the window to get me out of my shock to move out of the bed. It was a terrifying experience. Unfortunately, my roommates and I were not the most intuitive or wise 20-year-olds. We discussed the creepy event and chalked it off to "ghosts" living in our house.

More strange things started happening in the house after that episode with the night intruder. My two female roommates and I had framed baby pictures of ourselves on the mantle. We noticed one after another, the photos would disappear. Another example of a strange and unexplained occurrence was the theft of some recordings we took of the house. We had some college parties at our house that were definitely not edifying, but were certainly fun for people in their twenties. I owned a video camera (pre-smartphone era) and we loved to record things during the parties and watch the intoxicated shenanigans over breakfast the next day. One morning, we gathered to watch the recording of the prior evening's party, and the camera was where we left it, but the recorded tape was missing. The bag with all of our tapes was gone without a trace. We asked our friends if they were playing a joke on us, but nobody knew where the tapes had vanished.

About a month later, I was taking a nap on the couch around 10 p.m., which is a normal nap hour for people who live the night life of Miami. All of a sudden, the most bloodcurdling scream I have ever heard woke me. My roommate had stepped out of her bedroom and saw a strange man standing over me. He had a knife in his hand. My roommate came out and caught him, and he took off running through the window in our kitchen that was opened by him. I remember just screaming and seeing the Nike Swoosh of his tennis shoes fly out the window. All we could do was scream; words were not coming to us. I dropped the phone several times trying to call 911 because I was shaking so violently from the intrusion.

With all of the yelling, a neighbor came over to see what was going on. He said he saw a man on a bicycle ride down our carport from the back of the house on to the street. The man looked calm and collected and left our house as if he was supposed to be there.

The neighbor even noticed the bike he was on was one he had seen late at night by a tree in our yard on other occasions. He assumed it was one of our friends. The "ghost" that had been coming in and out of our house was actually a man that had intent to harm us, starting with me that evening.

Needless to say, I was traumatized. I left Miami shortly after to live with my parents for a while. The police had his DNA from the fingerprints on the window and blood that he shed from flying out the window. Months later, the Miami police department called me to let me know the man had been caught. His DNA matched in a case that had just happened. Tragically, the young woman in this case was not spared by the grace of God like I had been and was raped. I might not have been walking with Jesus then, but He was walking with me and protecting me. The sword of the Spirit (the Bible) was my armor, along with the prayers of my faithful mom. Because of this, I believe I was shielded from being a victim of a heinous crime through my roommate's alarm and presence.

For the word of God is living and active, sharper than any two-edged sword, piercing to the division of soul and of spirit, of joints and of marrow, and discerning the thoughts and intentions of the heart.– Hebrews 4:12 (ESV)

Another incident happened a couple of years later when I was living with a roommate again in a different house. That same Bible was still collecting dust in my bedroom. I had gone out with "friends" that were interested in setting me up with a new, cute guy in town. We all went out and had a good time. I had a couple of drinks and he offered to drive me home with his friend. I was not interested in him as more than a friend, and I just thought it was okay, since he was a friend of my friends. When we arrived to my house, he asked if he could use the bathroom. Innocently, I thought it was no big deal and allowed him to enter the house.

I showed him to the bathroom and he made a physical advance on me. I shoved him away letting him know I was not a "hook-up" kind of girl. He then forcefully grabbed me, pushed me into my bedroom, and threw me on my bed, physically attacking me as I tried to fight back. I was overpowered and terrified. All of a sudden, he screamed out in pain. He rolled off and I had a chance to grab a lamp, smash it over him, and escape outside. The greatest dog I will ever know, Lexi, my lab-pit mix, busted through the door and took a chunk out of my assaulter's leg. Again, the Lord was protecting me. Although I was violated and afraid, he was not able to rape me.

This experience led to more pain. I shared what had happened with my "friends," and I was met with disbelief. In fact, the guy that attacked me had a quick story of what a "crazy" girl I was, and that I was scorned because he was not interested in me and was making the attack up. Nobody believed me at the time. I did not have the wisdom to call the police that night and file a report. It was my word against his. My world became dark for a while after that. It was a difficult experience that I suppressed for many years. I kept it locked in a box of trauma, in a chamber of my memory and heart that was shut off until now. My #MeToo stories left wounds that Jesus has made into victory scars in the past couple of years through His healing power. They may seem "lighter" or "heavier" compared to other #MeToo stories shared by women and men worldwide, but they were terrifying and painful experiences none the less, like all these stories are.

Fifteen years later, I can see the one and only who kept me safe—Jesus. He did not let those men destroy me. It was frightening and terrible to go through, but God knew it would be a testimony one day. The divine intervention of my roommate and my dog in those situations were answers to prayer. They were a part of the story and purpose that God created for my life.

For the first time, I started my journey of reading through the Bible given to me seventeen years earlier. My life was changed, verse by verse, chapter by chapter, and book by book. This was the gaping hole in my faith as a Christian. Despite the years I devoted to God as my Savior, I had not done one key thing—spend time in HIS word. I found refuge in His word as it showed me the correct path to tread on. The Holy Spirit was speaking to me and still does today through the Word of God. Every morning, when I wake up for my quiet time with the Lord in my secret place, I am showered by His love, comfort, strength, and revelation. It is the most important time of the day. Falling in love with God's Word in 2017 was one of the best experiences of my life, right there with becoming a mother. The book of life, the greatest love story ever written to humanity, was writing a new story in my heart.

As I dove into the Bible, I had a hard time understanding what I was reading the first couple of months. The reading plan my church was doing is called the *Discipleship Reading Plan*. It is divided into monthly readings of New and Old Testament and then explores the book of Psalms, Proverbs, and Song of Solomon throughout the year. As I read through the Gospel, my heart for the Lord and all of his unconditional love grew tremendously, but the Old Testament was difficult for me to understand at first. I would read different versions to try and make sense of it, but I struggled. Fortunately, the Lord brought me a helper to keep me encouraged and to help me seek the Holy Spirit as I read to open my spiritual eyes. I am forever grateful to my friend and mighty prayer warrior, Matthew, for pouring into me and teaching me how to spend time in God's Word and how to let it sink in and transform me from the inside out.

As the summer approached, God's Word was making more and more sense. It was as if scripture was coming alive off of the pages, moving through my heart, mind, and spirit, and washing old thoughts out with the loving truth of God. The Lord was renewing my mind, heart, and spirit.

I was growing, and growing hungry for Jesus.

I spent the summer in prayer for prosperity. The Lord blessed me with a new living situation that was incredible. I had moved into a beautiful, spacious home in the lush Manoa Valley. The home is owned by a sweet friend and jiujitsu sister. Her family was relocated to the mainland, and she blessed James and I with an affordable rent in a place that was certainly out of this single-mama teacher's league. Although I knew I could cover the bills, it was still a stretch. I needed a financial miracle to help me clear debt and live within my means.

Spending the summer with family and time in the Bible, my mom had an idea to get an appraisal on the house I had bought in Jacksonville a few years before. The real estate market was doing really well in the area, and my mom believed that my house had appreciated. She felt that I would be able to get equity out of the home to pay off other loans and debt. As I spent time in prayer about this, the Lord was making moves. When the appraisal came back, we were elated. The house had more than doubled in value in three years. The house my family and I battled over buying ended up being one of my greatest financial blessings. It was a powerful confirmation to trust in the Lord when He is speaking. It was hard to go against my parents' wishes at the time in purchasing this house. I would not live in it, but I kept hearing the Lord tell me to go through with the deal. It took a few years to understand why. Once the house was refinanced, I was able to pay off all of my debt and start a savings for the first time as a single mother.

However, the first thing I did with the money was something that would grow me closer to God more than any other single experience thus far. I was a huge fan of the worship band *Jesus Culture* since my darkest hour when Jesus saved me years before, and they were doing a special conference in Sacramento in the beginning of 2018. I bought my tickets, booked my Airbnb, and was excited for a four-day journey with God at *Jesus Encounter*.

I continued to dig deep into God's word, as He was transforming me and convicting my heart of different things. I had attended Bible study at my pastor's house quite a few times, but "regular" attendance was a far stretch. In prayer, I heard from God about this. How was it that I had time and energy to pack my son up with dinner and head to the dojo to train jiujitsu twice a week at night, but it was too much to drive to Bible study and fellowship and grow in my faith? It was at this time that I decided that bible study came first. This meant that my twice-a-week jiujitsu practice would become once-a-week. I made the decision that honoring God and growing in His Word comes first.

The Lord also placed me into ministry in a way only He could. At church one Sunday, I saw this beautiful little blonde family in attendance that I had never seen before. The three kids were around my son's age. There was a woman there with them who appeared to be their mom. After a couple of weeks of seeing them, I heard from the Lord to befriend her. I am so thankful for making the choice to be obedient and introduce myself to her. My new sweet sister in Christ was in crisis. She was a believer who had grown up in the church with faithful parents. She was married for 13 years and had moved to Hawaii two months prior as a military spouse with her husband and three children. After a month of being in a far-off state (relocated from the East Coast), her husband dropped a bomb and told her he wanted a divorce. It was a devastating blow, and this mama was on her knees praying to the Lord to get her through this hell.

When the Lord gets us through hell and heals us, He puts people in our path that are walking what we walked out. I could speak life into my precious sister who was in despair because she could see that my son and I were doing well. Our story gave her that mustard seed of faith and hope she needed in her redeemer, Christ the Lord.

Tim and I walked a long and convoluted path to reach a place where we could find joy and peace and provide that for our son, although our family was broken. With God's help, we formed a cohesive co-parenting unit that benefits James in every way that is possible.

My friend saw the strength in me that is a unique strength to single moms. A strength that I know I could not walk out with confidence, grace, and wisdom without Jesus walking every step of the way with me. Seeing the hope in my broken friend's eyes almost made all the pain and suffering I had walked through okay, because I knew God was using it for a purpose. My dear sister was the first person I could see God move through with my story as a beacon of light from the Lord.

I watched my sister lean into God ferociously. The Bible, prayer, fellowship, and worship were the only answers my sister accepted. The transformation from a fragile, broken person to a radiating godly warrior with supernatural strength was miraculous. Her crown of glory from God as a daughter of the Most High King was impenetrable. This was one of the most inspiring things I have witnessed.

This first year reading through the Bible that had been with me for seventeen years moved my heart in many ways. The favors and blessings that came from this decision to make daily time in God's Word a priority filled me with a constant flow of peace and joy and revelation. Even through the tough days, I would find refuge in my Bible.

Chapter 10

Rising Raiza

---

*But you will receive power when the Holy Spirit
has come upon you, and you will be my witnesses
in Jerusalem and in all Judea and Samaria, and
to the end of the earth.*
- Acts 1:8 (ESV)

I n January 2018, my church was in its second year of reading through the Bible. I decided to gather a small group of women who were interested in reading through the Bible to meet together at a coffee shop down the street from my house in Manoa. Surprisingly, a couple of girlfriends from my dojo joined the Bible study. I was happy they would be there because I was so excited to share the word of God with them. When I entered the coffee shop, my young friend Kate was already there. I was delighted to see that her Bible was open to Matthew 7. She was reading these particular scriptures:

> *"Enter through the narrow gate; for the gate is wide
> and the way is broad that leads to destruction, and
> those who enter through it are many. How narrow
> is the gate and difficult the way that leads to life,
> and those who find it are few." Matthew 7:13 (Tree
> of Life Version)*

I said hello to Kate and got in line to order a coffee. That's when a loud sound went off in the coffee shop. It was every cell phone in the coffee shop receiving a text message at once. In Hawaii, we receive alert notifications if the weather is particularly bad, but on this day the weather was perfect. I wondered what the text message could be and I looked over at my friend. The color had drained from her face as she walked toward me with her phone... The coffee shop went silent. The alert on everyone's phone stated that there was an incoming ballistic missile threat to Hawaii, it advised residents to seek shelter, and concluded "This is not a drill."

Initially, I was shocked. I wondered if it was real. My friend looked as if she was about to cry. She was in a panic like the rest of the hundreds of thousands of Hawaii residents in that moment.

"What do we do now?" Kate asked.

"We will call our loved ones, and then we will pray," I said.

I immediately called my son's father to check on them. I told him to tell my son that I loved him. We decided we did not want to terrify our child in case this was a fluke. Next, I called my parents, and then I sent several text messages to my mighty prayer warriors on the mainland to pray for Hawaii.

After calling, I began a collective prayer. As I led the prayer in the coffee shop, I asked the Holy Spirit to be present with us there, to shield all of Hawaii and God's children there. I repented of my sins and was ready for God's will to be done. In that prayer time, I literally felt the anointing of the Holy Spirit stir inside of me. In the midst of that divine encounter, the Lord gave me a beautiful vision that is still very distinct in my mind today. I saw an enormous shield break through the clouds in the sky. As if the shield was coming straight from heaven. Light was shining through an opening in the middle, and there were rainbows everywhere. I felt even more anointed after having this vision, and it was as if God was laying a comforter of peace right on us in the middle of a terrifying moment. We waited inside the shelter of the store for more news. After about 20 minutes of waiting and searching media sites on our phones for any word to come about this threat, there was a tweet from U.S. Representative Tulsi Gabbard that stated it was a false alarm for Hawaii; there was no nuclear threat. It took 38 minutes to receive a second alert from officials on our phones that this was a false alarm. During that time, many people did crazy things. There were news reports of parents putting their children in drainage sewers. We also heard in the news about mass hysteria. Many believed these were their last moments alive.

This morning of January the 13th set the tone of my radical journey with Jesus for 2018. There is no feeling more amazing than escaping "death" and letting God's glory ignite a new level of zeal and passion for witnessing and sharing the Gospel. That moment of leading the prayer boldly in a public place, and knowing countless brothers and sisters in Hawaii were praying similar prayers, was a unique experience I will never forget. The chains of any kind of insecurity to pray in public and proclaim Jesus as the Lord and Savior in me were lifted that morning.

A couple of weeks later, I was set to travel to Sacramento for the "Jesus Culture Encounter Conference." I did not really know much about the conference, except that there would be amazing worship there. I had already watched a few of the speakers who were speaking at the conference preach on YouTube. However, I was most excited to see Lisa Bevere preach at the conference. She is an amazing woman of God who speaks and writes with great authority in Christ. I highly recommend watching one of her sermons on YouTube if you have not had the pleasure. The passion she stands in with Christ is so fierce that it can make a believer out of anyone.

I traveled to Sacramento and arrived in the middle of the night to a hostel. My Airbnb was not available until the second evening. I stayed at the Victorian Mansion HI in Sacramento that was built in 1885. The old architecture made it look haunted. I arrived at 1 a.m. and knocked on the door. While I waited for someone to open the door, I was a bit spooked. Then, a sweet young lady answered the door and showed me to my room. Even though I was concerned about the place being haunted, it turned out to be a comfortable stay, and I had a rather peaceful rest. When I woke up, I went down for a cup of coffee and found two women with their heads bowed in prayer at the table. As I got closer to them, I realized they were praying in Spanish.

When those two ladies got up from prayer, they saw me standing in the room. I said hello, and soon we were talking about our faith and God's mysterious power in our lives. As we talked, I realized that it was a divine connection. These women were faithful believers who worked in ministry and walked with strong intercessory gifts. The gift of intercession has to do with praying on behalf of others; it is a gift of the heart that God recognizes and honors. When we petition God in prayer from humble hearts, He hears us and answers according to His will and Word. One of them led a ministry and could sing as well. She could also translate and pray fluently in five languages. As we all talked and learned about one another, we also discussed the unbelievable miracles Christ had done and was doing in our lives. The entire conversation was very encouraging. These two ladies became my two new sisters in Christ. They prayed over me and it worked as the catalyst for an encounter weekend with God. I could have never dreamed this up. The Lord was working before me in HIS divine ways.

> *The Lord went before them, in a pillar of cloud during the day to lead them on the way, and in a pillar of fire during the night to give them light. So they could travel day and night. Exodus 13:21 (NIV)*

One of the women had two messages to deliver to me from the Lord that she heard while praying over me. One message was

"God had separated me from a godly man to grow and learn more about the Lord. But that He would be bringing the man back in my life, and it was sooner than I thought." The second word from God was *"I had a son with an anointing on his life, that our ministries would be interconnected and that he would lead many to Christ."* These words shook me. I was speechless and needed time to process what I had heard. These messages happened in prayer in the Spirit, but it felt as if God was speaking to me directly. There was so much anointing in that room. It was a tangible experience of the Holy Spirit's presence.

During the previous year, in 2017, while I was reading through the Bible for the first time, my friend Matthew was an encourager, teacher, and prayer warrior with me. When I was confused about the Bible (especially about the Old Testament), Matthew was there to help me understand. He taught me to pray before reading the Bible and to ask the Holy Spirit to speak to me before reading the Bible. As I followed his instructions and prayed before reading, it felt as if the words of God began to make sense to me. Words that were so confusing and hard to follow for years all of a sudden became clear and alive. The more I read, the more I wanted to read, there were times that reading the Bible was the only thing I desired to do.

Although I was already baptized before as a baby in the Catholic Church, my friend Matthew really encouraged me in 2017 to get baptized as an adult and be born again in Christ. There is a difference in being a baby and not really having your own free will to choose to follow Christ, and being an adult and making that public declaration that Jesus is your Lord and Savior in front of your church family. I was so blessed to get baptized by my pastors at the Wave Christian Fellowship. My brothers and sisters in Christ were there to witness this and hold me accountable and love me through the valleys to the victories. This act of baptism made me a new person. My spirit was made new. The Holy Spirit was no longer just upon me, protecting me, whispering things, and guiding me. It was now living inside me, as I was now ready to be used to see wonders, signs, miracles, deliverances, and healings happen in the name of Jesus. I became His vessel through the act of faith that is baptism.

Matthew had moved to Florida in the end of 2017. He was ready to be on the East Coast and be closer to his family after spending so many years in Hawaii. I was sad to lose such a great friend and spiritual leader in my life, but I was also glad he was going where God was leading him. When those two ladies in Sacramento gave me that word in prayer, [Matthew] was the one who came to mind at once. Who knew? Maybe our paths would cross again one year. This prayer gathering had me fully anticipating God to do something in me that weekend at Jesus Culture Encounter.

The conference started with rocking praise and worship by Elevation Worship Band. It was incredible being in a packed venue with so many believers singing and dancing and praising God. The presence of God was so thick that I felt as if the atmosphere even looked different. Lights, colors, smiles, hands raised to God—all of it was brighter and full of life. There is something so special that happens when thousands unite to pursue one thing—God's presence. Bill Johnson was the speaker on the first night. I heard before that his messages were anointed. After an incredible word from God, I saw miracles in the form of healing. Something I had never seen before. People were being healed of physical ailments all around me. Ear pain, joint pain, stomach issues, growths on body parts were all being healed in the name of Jesus. People who had been suffering from so many physical things were all weeping tears of joy around me. My faith was elevated that evening. It was just the preface to how the entire weekend would go.

I went back to my Airbnb with the fire of God in me still burning. I call it the Jesus stoke. This was the first time I had experienced this level of God's presence. I could barely sleep that night; I was dancing around the Airbnb like a wild woman to worship music, and then I started to write. I wrote the message from God I was hearing all night long. I even drew things, which surprised me since I do not draw, as in *at all*. I slept only a couple of hours, but woke up fully rested and alert. I was not hungry for food. I was hungry for more of God's presence.

I went back to the venue and was there for every praise and worship and every speaker. It was a complete download of so much biblical revelation into my heart, mind and soul. My spirit was being fed. Without any intentional planning my body was physically fasting. I had to remind myself to drink water, but there was no way I could eat food. The experience of sitting in the audience of the live recording of the Jesus Culture's latest album "Living with a Fire," singing, crying, and experiencing God in such a tangible way is still indescribable for me. The music of Jesus Culture worship band had saved me before from taking my life years before when I was in the darkest valley, and here I was in the audience, singing along with them. God had taken me from being a victim to be a victor. His glory was raining down on me.

I was walking in with the crowd to the venue to listen to Lisa Bevere's message that evening, and was unexpectedly pulled aside. I was immediately concerned that I had violated some sort of rule such as the dress code or had the wrong wrist band on, but this was not the case at all. The usher that pulled me from the large crowd walking in looked at me with the kindest eyes I have ever seen and said, *"This message will bless you very much. You will be used mightily by God. He sees your heart for others."*

I was taken to John 4 with the Samaritan woman at the well. The Samaritans were known as the "dirty" people, and women were half-citizens at that time. The disciples were shocked that Jesus was even speaking to her. The voices of the world sought to undermine her value and worth but not Jesus. He told her about her life. He said to her, "I see you. You do not have to wait; your Messiah is here."

My jaw dropped, and I was filled with a sense I had never experienced. It was the first time I really felt and knew without a doubt that God knew me like nobody else ever could. He knew me better than I knew myself. He had a great purpose and plan for my life. As I listened to Lisa Bevere preach and teach about sexual immorality and God's truth, I felt the chains that had been holding me captive for so many years of dating vanish. I could never get my virginity back, but I could live in recovered virtue. I could still live with purity. Those words healed my heart, and as the praise and worship closed the evening out, I heard from the Lord, "*You have been healed, now go and see many others healed. Be bold and fearless, my daughter!*"

Again, I did not sleep much that night. The Holy Spirit was speaking to me, and I could not stop writing it all down that night. When the morning came, I realized that it was the last day of the Encounter Conference. I felt I had even more energy than I had when I arrived. I had not slept, I had not eaten food, I was forcing myself to drink water, but I was still full and satisfied. The Holy Spirit was pouring into and onto me. The Lord was giving me prophetic words for some of my sisters in Christ. He was showing me new life and babies for some, and also some very tough seasons for others. I believe He showed me this to be an encourager and prayer warrior for my sisters as they walked through the season ahead.

The last message of the conference was one on "Awakening" given by Banning Liebscher. This message was filled with God's glory and power. The time when the church would become the center of culture again was the call the Lord placed on the lead pastor of Jesus Culture. This was a mighty call indeed. To see this happen, God's children must be in His presence. Victory and breakthroughs are amazing, but God's presence in a room of five people or a stadium of thousands is what we will seek. This will lead us to "awakening."

As the conference came to an end that evening, it was like the day of Pentecost. The Holy Spirit had come and poured out on all of His children. I walked out and felt as if I was walking on clouds. It was night time, but everything was still so bright. I saw hundreds of believers praying in groups all over the venue and on the streets of Sacramento. I had never seen anything like this. *"On earth, as it is in heaven"* was all I could think of at that moment.

I heard the Lord telling me to pray with someone. I walked around and kept walking to groups of people asking "God, here? Pray with these people?" None of the groups were calling me to pray. I decided to call for my Uber and give myself some pressure to find the person or group God wanted me to pray with. Ten minutes went by, and I had not prayed. My Uber arrived, and I felt defeated.

I stepped into the car and said to myself, *"Enemy, you will not take this moment from me. Jesus is here and I will not feel like a disappointment for not praying."* Then my super-friendly Uber driver inquired about what was going on with all of the people praying. She was curious and excited to know. We chatted all the way to the house, and I told her all about the conference and what the Lord was doing. She shared how she was a believer but had not gone to church in years. She told me about how she had lived in Hawaii and volunteered for a ministry on the North Shore that helped rescue victims of sex trafficking and relocate them to Oakland, where they would be supported in their restoration process. I could feel her spirit starting to awaken in the middle of our conversation on the way back to my Airbnb.

When we arrived at the house, I asked her if I could pray for her. She responded, *"I was hoping you would ask."*

It was awesome to pour that Holy Spirit fire from the conference out onto another sister who was hindered in her walk with

God. *"Take that, enemy!"* was all I could think as I danced my way in the Spirit to bed.

As soon as I arrived back to Oahu from that trip, I turned on my cell phone in the airport. I had received a text message from Matthew.

Matthew: Hey, I want to hear about your Encounter Weekend.

Me: Sure, I will call you when I get home.

Matthew: I want to hear in person.

Me: What? I am in Hawaii, you live in Florida.

Matthew: I moved back this week.

Me: What??? Why didn't you tell me you were moving back?

Matthew: I didn't want to interrupt your time with the Lord.

I was blown away; my new sister who had the prophetic word about a godly man coming back into my life had been very accurate. When I reached out to her on social media to tell her, she said she knew. She saw him on a plane. He had been traveling from Florida to Hawaii the day she gave me that word from God.

Chapter 11

Walking Acts Out

This is what I will do in the last days-I will
pour out my Spirit on everybody and cause
your sons and daughters to prophesy, and
your young men will see visions, and your old
men will experience dreams from God. The Holy
Spirit will come upon all my servants, men and
women alike, and they will prophesy
—Acts 2:17 (Passion Translation)

Coming back to Hawaii from that trip with God was a whirlwind. It is hard to describe an encounter with God like that.
That experience was a defining lifetime memory. It was as if my
heart was set on fire to see God move more powerfully and consistently in and through my life. I saw miracles happen with my own
eyes and heard God speak to me. There were two journals full of
messages, notes, and drawings that I brought home. Much of it did
not make sense at the time. As the year progressed, more and more
things from these journals became clearer. Some pieces of the prophetic words God gave me for my life, and those in my life—even
larger visions—began to come together. Shawn Bolz, a prophet
of Christ, gave me two scriptures when I met him in Sacramento.
They were Isaiah 22:22 and Ephesians 3:20.

> *Isaiah 22:22 I will give him the key to the house of David—the highest position in the royal court. When he opens doors, no one will be able to close them; when he closes doors, no one will be able to open them. (NLT)*

> *Ephesians 3:20 Now all glory to God, who is able, through his mighty power at work within us, to accomplish infinitely more than we might ask or think. (NLT)*

These scriptures were powerful, but what did they mean? It is a divine mystery when hearing sound bites from God. All I knew at the time was that I was changed forever and more excited about life than I had ever been. The bold spirit that had always defined me in my twenties was refreshed and renewed with the Word of God as my miraculous adventures with Jesus continued in new ways.

I heard the Lord tell me to speak and see women healed by Jesus like HE healed me at the conference. What did God mean? For my sweet friend who walked through her divorce with such strength and grace, my story was one of hope that she could lean on through the darkness. Was I to start a ministry for single moms? Broken hearts? I was not sure, but I was ready to act. I spoke with some of my sisters in Christ and decided to host my first ministry event at my house. A book swap for women. Some were moms; some were not. Some were believers, some were not. There is a Youth With a Mission (YWAM) Base Camp in my neighborhood, and I am friends with the leaders there. A few of the girls volunteered to babysit kids for the Book Swap night. It was a special evening and I could feel God's presence. Beautiful women of many different ages and backgrounds got to know one another while eating and sharing. There was even an opportunity for me to share my radical testimony of Christ saving me for the first time with a group of women who knew me.

After the first Book Swap I thought, *"Well, Lord this must be what you want me to do. Host a monthly evening for women and just put Christ on display."* I invited a group of women the next month to come again. This time I felt a little overwhelmed. There were a lot of things happening in my personal life and many women that came before did not respond to the invitation or just did not show up. It was a much smaller group of women, but a fruitful evening nonetheless. We talked, shared, and prayed together. I learned that evening that the Lord will call the people who are supposed to be present. My job is to pray and invite. God has a purpose in all things. The gospel of Matthew states*: "Where two or three are gathered in my name, there I am with them." Matthew 18:20.* God is present. It never matters the amount of people who show up to any ministry event or meeting; what matters is God's presence.

After the second Book Swap, I spent time praying to the Lord. Was this His will for me to continue this monthly? Was this a ministry God wanted for me?

I heard from the Lord, "Don't rush and miss the target."

What did that mean? "Miss the target?" Was I not meant to minister to women? Through my prayer time and mediation on scripture, I realized that I was rushing because it is my goal-oriented personality to get things done, but maybe I was not ready. There was so much confusion in my mind about this, and I felt stressed preparing for another Book Swap. That uneasiness was a sign to me from God that this might not be what His purpose was for me. Maybe I needed more time to prepare for what God was calling me into? I would continue searching and seeking the Lord to reveal what it was that He wanted me to do.

After reading every Lisa Bevere book I could get my hands on, I started reading another book I picked up at Encounter Conference in Sacramento: *Rooted: The Hidden Places Where God Develops*

You by Banning Liebscher. This book was transformative and, of course, at such a divine time, as I was searching for answers to what it was that God was calling me to do. I knew it was something that would set my soul ablaze, but had not figured out what it was yet. As I read through this book, I began to understand the life of King David and how God grew him patiently, quietly developing deep roots in his soul and spirit long before David would wear the crown as King of Israel. It was such an encouraging read, as I realized I needed to surrender to God and not try to "figure out" what it was that He was calling me to do. The Lord wanted personal time with me, in the secret place of the mornings, afternoons, evenings, and all the pockets of time He would make for us. It was supernatural, as if God was slowing time and my schedule in ways during these months to just soak in His Word and presence.

> *He who dwells in the secret place of the Most High*
> *shall abide under the shadow of the Almighty. I will*
> *say of the Lord, "He is my refuge and my fortress;*
> *My God, in Him I will trust." Psalm 91:1-2 (NKJV)*

My time with God included reading and meditating on the Bible, praying, and journaling. It included time in worship as I sang to Jesus. This precious time was so crucial in my spiritual journey. It was time to understand God's character and heart at much deeper levels. It was time to allow His word to resonate in my soul, transform my spirit, and remove one stone after another from my heart. He was creating a new version of a woman after God's heart.

A month later, on social media, a friend from church had posted a donation page for her birthday. It was for a local nonprofit with a mission to end sex trafficking of minors in Hawaii. I immediately thought back to the Uber driver in Sacramento that shared her heart about serving in this fight against trafficking in Hawaii, and how her testimony touched my heart. I heard about girls being sold repeatedly for sex, but I thought maybe it was just a problem overseas, not so much in the United States. I donated and checked out the website of the nonprofit. It looked interesting, and with my fourteen years as a teacher of at-risk youth, I was moved to learn more about this social problem. They had a volunteer training a couple weeks away. I signed up and invited a sweet friend, Kylie, to join me. We were both interested in learning more. We had no idea how this evening would wreck our hearts in a tremendous way.

I cried during the education presentation. It was eye-opening, informative, and unbelievable. It was not normal tears. I wept. God showed me visions of former students, girls that showed signs of being abused, but would never confide fully in adults at school. It never occurred to me that someone could be profiting off selling these students. As a teacher, I always tried to connect and make relationships with these students that emotionally seemed so sad, isolated, and withdrawn. They had sullen faces, often with their heads on their desks, and they rarely completed assignments, and their condition would break my heart. The derogatory names these girls were given by their peers for their promiscuousness were devastating. Even the stench from some of their untreated sexually transmitted diseases would be profound in the classroom. For some of these girls, I would see small changes, and I helped them break through walls by counseling them. I would try to find community resources, and even took some to doctor's appointments for help. But for the majority, they would disappear and never come back to school. All of the girls that flashed in a vision that evening had been students that just never came back. Where were they? The ignorance I lived in as a teacher shocked my soul. I cried myself to sleep that night like never before.

A short time later, Jesus Culture had reached out to me to do a testimony interview with Kim Walker-Smith. During the Encounter weekend in Sacramento, I posted something on social media. A friend who I met in Jacksonville years before read my post. It turned out she was now a marketing director for Jesus Culture. She reached out to me at the conference to share my testimony live on Jesus Culture social media platform. The first time I shared my full testimony of Jesus saving my life was before a live audience of a million, and now Jesus Culture wanted to do a more formal interview of this miraculous testimony. The very voice from the Lord that sang His praises during my darkest suicidal moments was going to interview me. I was blown away at God's plans. As I spoke with Kim through video conferencing, I felt as if I was speaking to a good friend, a sister in Christ who was also a mother of young children and balancing life, work, and ministry. It was a special hour that brought even more healing to my story of single parenthood. The Lord's village was extending globally for my son and I.

The education presentation on trafficking was at the forefront of my mind for weeks. I kept praying and asking God how He saw me being used in the sex-trafficking fight. All of my years of teaching at-risk youth had been equipping me in understanding just how vulnerable this population is to this heinous crime, but I wondered what role God wanted me to play in ending this savagery. I heard back from the Lord to *"get educated, and to keep speaking. A voice for the voiceless. Wake my children up."* This is a word from God I have heard repeatedly in prayer since my first volunteer training. I did just that. I read and researched on the subject. I watched many documentaries. I went into a dark vortex of truth. During these few weeks of extensive training and research, it was hard to function with joy in my life. I was starting a new job at a precious elementary school with my son in attendance; an incredible opportunity and answer to prayer. There were so many divine beautiful things happening in my personal life, yet this heavy burden of girls, women, and boys being sold for sex over and over right there in my own backyard made it so hard to be at peace in the moment. God was stirring my spirit. *"Wake my children up"* was on repeat in my mind.

At church, I went up to the altar call and received anointed oil and prayer from my pastors. I needed the Lord to bring comfort to my breaking heart for these victims. It is impossible to unknow what we learn. Everything involved with the trafficking of humans is as evil and inhumane as it gets here on Earth. There was a great purpose in the Lord exposing me to this and calling me to rise up for these captives. He wanted me to be a voice for the voiceless. After time in prayer at church and in the Word of God, my peace was starting to return. I was activated to move.

The Lord wanted me to go there in the darkness and know the truth. He set my heart on fire to be a warrior for this cause and to see the sex trafficking of humans end, especially minors. My quiet, special hours and days with the God resting all spring and summer were times of equipping. This was a time of understanding spiritual armor and putting it on daily. Also, it was imperative in understanding how the Word of God was my weapon, the most powerful tool in this fight to set His captives free. Like King David, Jesus was ready to use me, and I was His surrendered vessel in this war against sex trafficking.

I went to work all fall, volunteering at events, speaking, presenting to groups in the community, and even working with a fantastic small business, Kekoa Collective, to see the jiujitsu community begin to rise up against this crime as well. The powerful grappling community is the complete opposite of how traffickers operate. Professors empower girls and women to understand their bodies in the area of self-defense and how to use their bodies as weapons. It is a priceless tool that gives girls and women a sense of value and confidence. The boys and men who train jiujitsu learn honor, respect, and discipline in a way that the fast-paced culture of the world today is trying to tear down.

Today, I continue to share with the jiujitsu and Christian communities about this crime, and they are shocked that it is happening everywhere, even in the cities they live in. Many are ready to move into action against this world-wide epidemic. A future jiujitsu tournament in Hawaii is being planned to bring awareness and support to a local nonprofit with the mission to end sex trafficking and restore minors that are victims of this crime. The Lord has even made many divine connections that have led me to meeting and speaking with leaders of churches in Hawaii. God wants more and more of His children to understand this crime, prevent it, see captives set free, and see buyers and traffickers healed and restored. Jesus can and will do this. He is activating His body globally for this purpose.

Just like an alcoholic or a drug addict, a sex and porn addict can be healed by the blood of Christ and fully restored. We, the church, can be witnesses and see this deliverance to stop the demand. Jesus is that powerful. He can radically encounter a trafficker and change his or her heart to stop selling humans, just like Saul had an encounter with Jesus on the road to Damascus while he was persecuting Christians. These traffickers can be healed in prison, where they belong. This type of restoration requires action from the church, mighty intercession, and movement in the name of Jesus. I am praying that God uses me and other bold warriors everywhere to keep activating more boldness and movement in this fight. This is a fight against evil that will take a mighty army.

As the Lord moves me deeper into this journey of ministry and deliverance, I am so grateful for all HIS protection, love, mercy, and GRACE that has gotten me here today. From a heartbroken, shattered, suicidal pregnant woman in despair to a warrior of the Lord walking mightily with Jesus in recovered virtue. Who knows what God has in store for my personal life? Maybe I am called to be a single woman intimately connected to Jesus until the day I go home to the Lord. Maybe a godly warrior will pursue me one day. Either way, I am at peace and filled with joy that only comes from God. And that is the most precious part to this story. His GRACE is sufficient. The breakthrough of the world's destructive cycle of "hook up, shack up, break up, repeat" is finished in my life, by the blood of the Lamb. If I look to the left or right and see a man running at my pace or faster after Christ, he just might get my attention. Until that moment, I will keep my eyes fixed on my rescuer, Jesus Christ, the lover of my soul.

> *Never doubt God's mighty power to work in you and accomplish all this. He will achieve infinitely more than your greatest request, your most unbelievable dream and exceed your wildest imagination! He will outdo them all, for his miraculous power constantly energizes you.–Ephesians 3:20 (Passion Translation)*

About the Author

R aiza Garcia is a single mom of a young boy and a special
education teacher for 14 years in Hawaii and Florida. She
serves in her local church and in ministries that help at-risk youth
when she is not playing with her son or training Jiu Jitsu. She has
a heart to see the church and martial arts community rise up for
the most vulnerable youth in our communities that are in the child
welfare system.

CPSIA information can be obtained
at www.ICGtesting.com
Printed in the USA
FFHW020325160519
52495370-57921FF

9 781545 667330